How To Profit From Prophets

Sermons
For Advent
And Christmas

Maurice A. Fetty

CSS Publishing Company, Inc., Lima, Ohio

HOW TO PROFIT FROM PROPHETS

Copyright © 1998 by
CSS Publishing Company, Inc.
Lima, Ohio

All rights reserved. No part of this publication may be reproduced in any manner whatsoever without the prior permission of the publisher, except in the case of brief quotations embodied in critical articles and reviews. Inquiries should be addressed to: Permissions, CSS Publishing Company, Inc., P.O. Box 4503, Lima, Ohio 45802-4503.

Scripture quotations are from the *Revised Standard Version of the Bible*, copyrighted 1946, 1952 ©, 1971, 1973, by the Division of Christian Education of the National Council of the Churches of Christ in the USA. Used by permission.

"Choose Something Like A Star" and "Come In" from THE POETRY OF ROBERT FROST, edited by Edward Connery Lathem, Copyright 1942 by Robert Frost, © 1970, 1977 by Lesley Frost Ballantine, Copyright 1949, © 1969 by Henry Holt and Company, Inc., © 1997 by Edward Connery Lathem. Reprinted by permission of Henry Holt and Company, Inc.

Library of Congress Cataloging-in-Publication Data

Fetty, Maurice A., 1936
   How to profit from prophets : sermons for Advent and Christmas / Maurice A. Fetty
     p. cm.
   ISBN 978-0-7880-1277-8
   1. Advent sermons. 2. Bible. O.T. Prophets—Sermons. 3. Christmas—Sermons. 4. Sermons, American. I. Title.
BV40.F47   1998
252'.61—dc21   98-9386
                                                                                             CIP

This book is available in the following formats, listed by ISBN:
   0-7880-1277-0   Book
   0-7880-1278-9   IBM
   0-7880-1279-7   MAC
   0-7880-1280-0   Sermon Prep

PRINTED IN U.S.A.

To My Brothers and Sisters:

Gordon L. Fetty

Lowell L. Fetty

Kathleen Fetty Holst

Connie Fetty Keck

Preface

Advent appropriately begins the Christian year announcing the repeated coming of the Lord into human history. If God appeared to Abraham, Isaac, and Jacob, he also manifested himself in Moses, and most especially in the inspired prophets, chief of whom was, of course, Jesus, the son of God.

The prophets remind us that God's ways and thoughts always are higher than our ways and thoughts. Themselves often caught up in ecstatic visions, the prophets point us to mysteries and realities greater than our rational power to comprehend. We "profit most from prophets" in the Advent-Christmas season when they make us aware that in our worship, we are not dealing just with ourselves, but with Another, who comes to us to encourage us, to strengthen and heal us, and to make us whole. The good news is this; not only has he come to us, he comes to us again and again for our profit.

Table Of Contents

Chapter 1   9
How To Profit From Prophets
Luke 1:76

Chapter 2   15
Why Prophets Get Under Our Skin
Luke 3:9

Chapter 3   23
Someone Greater Than A Prophet
Luke 1:33

Chapter 4   31
The Long Loneliness
Romans 13:11-12

Chapter 5   39
A Voice To Be Heard
John 1:23

Chapter 6   49
The Unexpected Universe
Matthew 11:4-6

Chapter 7   59
The Star Thrower
Matthew 2:9-10

Chapter 8   69
The Inner Galaxy
Luke 2:6-7

Chapter 9   79
The Second Naiveté:
    Babies, Angels, Shepherds, And God
Philippians 2:8

Bibliography   87

Chapter 1
How To Profit From Prophets

> *"And you, child, will be called the prophet of the Most High; for you will go before the Lord to prepare his ways...."*
> — Luke 1:76

Many would claim the profit motive to be one of the stronger motives of our humanity. Though purists may snub their noses at it, and socialists may sneer at it, capitalists say profit and the profit motive are the driving force of any successful economy.

Welfare recipients might criticize the high profits of some persons and businesses. But those same persons and businesses would gladly quote former British Prime Minister Margaret Thatcher that any welfare system presupposes that someone, somewhere, is producing wealth to make the welfare payments. And you cannot produce wealth without making a profit. The great labor leader Samuel Gompers said, "The worst crime against working people is a company which fails to operate at a profit."

Most all of us hope to profit from business or profession or investments, but in the Advent Season we are asked to consider how we might profit from the prophets of God. If, in the financial world, profit means gain against costs, success against failure, and advancement against retreat, in the biblical domain the profit we might seek and expect from the prophets may well be of a different kind.

It is true, of course, that a number of popular religious leaders of today promise wealth and success as a by-product of religion. It is true, of course, that even in some of the biblical writings themselves, it is thought that if one is righteous one will be wealthy, and that, therefore, poverty must be a sign of the disfavor of God.

But the great biblical prophets move beyond those enticing and troubling words of false prophecy to give us a profit more enduring, more important, more successful in the long sweep of history.

Both the ancient world and the modern cherish wisdom, wealth, offspring, and power, says Abraham Heschel in his excellent book, *The Prophets*. There is deep in our hearts, says Heschel, "the temptation to worship the imposing, the illustrious and the ostentatious" (p. 8).

However, the luminous and explosive words of the prophet rivet our attention on the deeper dimensions of faith and the higher issues of morality and human destiny. Profits on Wall Street are admirable, but the stock market will, as J. P. Morgan put it, fluctuate.

Not so the steadfast will of God. And he who would profit most will heed the words of the prophets.

I

How can we profit from the prophets? John the Baptist was one of the greatest of the prophets. He was the new Elijah, said Mary. This new Elijah has come, says Zechariah, his father, **to give knowledge of salvation.**

The word *salvation* means wholeness or completeness of life, a life that encompasses the wide range of health and longevity, a life that is devoid of spiritual tumors and psychological fractures. It is a life of balanced tensions and wholesome outlook.

Just where does one get a knowledge of salvation like that? The customary places we look are in fame and power, position and wealth, recognition and success. Yet, the whole world knows wealthy people who are miserable, famous people who are hopeless drug addicts, and powerful people, like a Saddam Hussein, who are sadistic and brutal beyond belief.

Where might we look for salvation? To the medical and psychological worlds, of course. Without question we have been healed with surgery and drugs and medical technology and psychological insights and counseling. Who can deny the helpfulness of therapy and surgery? Many of us have profited enormously from them.

Yet the prophets call us to a greater knowledge of a salvation that comes by way of forgiveness of sins. Prophets do have a way of pointing out our sins, of excoriating our pride and immorality, of flushing out the deceitful and hypocritical elements of our soul. Like Nathan of old, pointing his trembling finger at King David, so they, in fearless voice and fierce demeanor point the finger at us and say, "Thou art the man. Thou art the woman."

But once the judgment is made and our contrition is noted, the prophets point to the tender mercies of God, and affirm that his kindness is greater than his wrath, that his love prevails over his judgment. It is this message of acceptance and forgiveness we can receive from God alone which gives us such profit.

II

Another way the prophets give us profit is **to give light to those who sit in darkness.**

There are at least two kinds of darkness. One is the darkness of ignorance and the other is the darkness of despair. And the prophets can and do give light for both.

Consider the matter of ignorance. Read the magnificent poetry and powerful prose sermons of the great prophets. Unlike some who equate religion with ignorance, and religious leaders with dogmatic rigidity, the prophets' words tingle with insight and vibrate with shimmering revelations. Scorning provincial mind-sets and bursting the bonds of smugness, the prophets always push us out of our stuffy conceits into new realities.

We profit from prophets because they urge us to push beyond the boundaries of what is comfortably known to the challenging unknown. If we are engrossed with narrow nationalism, they call us to an enlightened universalism. If we are self-centered, myopic, and defensive, they urge us to be considerate of others, to be farsighted and to take the offensive in actualizing the new realities. Instead of regressive, they are progressive.

However, the prophets know that darkness is more than ignorance and narrowness of mind. Darkness also can be a state of the soul, a malady of the heart. And if most of us struggle from time to time with ignorance, perhaps even more of us struggle with discouragement, despair, and depression.

But the prophets help us here, says Zechariah, because they give light to those who sit in the shadow of death. And what else are discouragement, despair, and depression but shadows of death?

Add to that disease and the threat of physical death itself and we have plenty to worry about.

And yet, it is the prophets who remind us again that the light of God is brighter than all our darkness and that the power of God is greater than all our weakness. If the Psalmist says, "The Lord is my light and salvation," the great prophet Isaiah affirms, "The people who walked in darkness have seen a great light; those who dwelt in a land of deep darkness, on them has light shined." Therefore, says Isaiah, "Thou hast multiplied the nation, thou hast increased its joy" (9:2-3).

Indeed God has. Through his prophets we are encouraged to have hope beyond all our despair and discouragement and death. God lightens even the darkness of death with the hope of life and light eternal.

III

But there is even more profit from the prophets. **They guide our feet in the way of peace.**

It is well-known we men hate to ask for directions. A secretary brought in a cartoon the other day which said Moses and the Israelites wouldn't have wandered around in the wilderness for forty years if Moses had been willing to ask for directions! And the prophets would remind us that humanity wouldn't be wandering around in the wilderness of violence and warmongering for so long if we would be more willing to ask for directions.

Of course we want the right directions, or do we? Amos and Isaiah and Jeremiah gave the right directions but they were ignored, to the great peril of national leaders. Jesus lamented that some prophets came fasting and no one would fast, others came eating and dancing and no one would eat and dance. When the prophets came with the way of God to guide us, we often persecuted them, ridiculed them, or even killed them. We'll do it our way, thank you.

And yet prophets like John the Baptist come out of their wilderness solitude with a message that rings true above the cacophony of the madding crowd and penetrates to a reality deeper than the frothy clamor of public opinion polls. It is the voice of the Eternal that becomes audible through their voice, the invisible One made visible through their moral transparency. Isn't it comforting to know that God has not left himself without witness? If we are willing to ask for directions, he does guide us in the way of peace.

The dividends from stocks and bonds are good. Increased business here and around the world can mean a better life for all. Real estate once again may appreciate to yield a good profit. But the profits from the prophets are even better, giving success to the soul, enlightenment to the mind, and hope for our troubled spirits. After all, what does it profit us if we gain the world and lose our souls? Always and forever the prophets bring salvation to the soul. And there is no greater profit than that!

Prayer

Almighty God, Spirit of the universe, in whose life all living things receive their heartbeat and in whose mind all thoughtful beings find their true home, we worship and adore you. You have given us voices to speak of your glory, souls to feel your love, and ears to hear of wonders too grand and mighty to comprehend. We thank you for your panoply of splendor.

Look kindly upon us as we bow in your presence, and receive us not so much as the people we are, but as the people we want to be. The visions we have, the ideals we embrace, and the goals for which we strive seem often to recede as we approach them, and the things we know we should have done seem never quite to be accomplished. Forgive us when we fall short, especially of the moral demands you place in our consciences.

The world is very much with us in buying and selling, working hard to get ahead and even winning at the money game. Grant that the things we see and possess may never capture our souls. Save us from the compulsions of greed and the anxieties of fear. Help us to relax into your grace and to focus on your eternal truth. For you are the sun and we the satellites, and in you we have our light and life. Renew us and refresh us we pray, that we might gladly do your will in all our living. Through Jesus Christ our Lord. Amen.

Chapter 2

Why Prophets Get Under Our Skin

"Even now the axe is laid to the root of the trees; every tree therefore that does not bear good fruit is cut down and thrown into the fire." — Luke 3:9

To tell you the truth, you might not like him if you met him. Chances are you would not invite him for cocktails at the club or for dinner at home with some of your prestigious friends. The likelihood is your children would think him curious and your teenagers would scorn him as not worth an autograph. The tabloids might attempt to puff him up as an oddity or curiosity piece for the sake of profit. But the respectable newspapers might think the news he had was not fit to print. I speak, of course, of John the Baptist.

After a long silence in the unique and influential strain of biblical prophets, John the Baptist appeared in the sparsely settled Jordan River valley preaching a startling message of judgment and repentance. Ascetic, gaunt, austere, and uncompromising, he resembled the austere severity of the wilderness where he sounded forth his message which has rebounded through the corridors of history for twenty centuries.

No street corner prophet this. No televangelist con artist, this prophet. No panderer after the sympathies of the rich and famous. No sycophant of the elite and powerful, this man. This man was a man of God — fierce, unyielding, piercing, penetrating, forthright, and forceful.

He sought no coveted memberships in elite organizations. He asked no favor of those in power and never fawned over those with position. Instead, the rich and famous left the comforts of their homes and clubs to come to the Jordan wilderness to hear him.

He was a novelty to be sure, and even King Herod went to hear him, only to have his ears singed with fiery rebuke and his heart pierced through with the living word of God. John had his day with Herod; but, of course, Herod later had his day with John, beheading him, and presenting the head on a platter to jealous and fearful Herodias.

Politicians may hold a finger to the political winds to set the sails of their political fortunes for a political safe haven, but not prophets. Politicians may take opinion polls to ascertain the direction of the political parade so as to get in front of it to appear as leaders, but not prophets. Politicians may speak with a forked tongue and out of both sides of their mouths, but not prophets. They tell it like it is, like it or not. And we usually don't. That's why we scorn them, keep them in the wilderness or lock them up or kill them if they get too close.

Let's kill the prophet Elijah, said Queen Jezebel to King Ahab nine centuries before Christ. Go back down south and preach there, the high priest Amaziah told the lonely and rustic Amos seven and a half centuries before Christ. Throw Jeremiah in the cistern, said King Zedekiah six centuries before Christ, because he never says anything good about me. But that's because there was nothing good to say.

These prophets, these brave, lonely, powerful, penetrating prophets. We have a strange, reluctant admiration for them, even if we do ignore them, ostracize them, persecute them, even kill them. Yet we have to deal with them, especially John the Baptist, because they are always getting under our skin. Why is that?

I

For one thing, **they criticize our background.**

In 1970, my wife and I went to Australia, where we stayed for about three weeks. The magnet that drew us there was a World Church Convention as well as our interest in the country itself. We stayed in hotels in some places. But at other times we were privileged to stay with Australian citizens in their homes. And while in their homes, there was one thing we didn't do; we didn't inquire into their background.

And why? Because, as many know, for a period of time Great Britain used Australia as a dumping ground for British criminals and other malcontents. Were you convicted in the British courts? Then it's either prison or Australia. Many had the good sense to choose Australia!

John the Baptist, knowing the background of many Australians, might have left them alone if they had the good sense to remain humble about themselves because of their background. But John knew most people didn't do that. He well knew that most people, in their anxiety of nothingness, and their craving for somethingness, begin to put undue pride in their background. They strive to develop a socially acceptable pedigree that will look good on the resumé and the club application.

But God, says fearless John, is more concerned about fruits than roots. God is more interested in where you are going than where you came from. He is more focused on what contribution you are going to make to society than on whether you grew up in the right neighborhood with the right parents and right schools on your resumé. If you are content to justify your life by bragging about your father and grandfather, God's prophet strips you of the family coat of arms and asks what you, in your time and place in history, will do for the kingdom of God. When it comes to faith and faithful living, God has no grandchildren. Each of us has to stand on our own.

Is it any wonder a lot of people wanted to see John dead? To the ancestrally elite and the religiously impeccable he was scathing. "You low-down, wriggling snake in the grass, who warned you to flee the wrath to come?" John knew there was nothing more obnoxious in the nostrils of God than puffy pride not only in ancestral lineage, but in religious heritage. That is why all of us handle John with fear and hear his message with trepidation. He gets under the skin of our conceit and pride — powerfully.

II

Another reason prophets get under our skin is because they **ask us to share our wealth**.

Oh, I know John's advice for a person with two tunics to share one of them with him who had none is simplistic and personalistic. To be sure, even Jesus' advice to share a cup of cold water with the thirsty and some food and clothing with the needy sounds too easy in view of the crunching, grinding poverty so prevalent in much of today's world.

However, both John and Jesus had something greater in mind than cleaning our closets of old clothes for the poor to make room for the new we bought at recent sales. Both were suggesting something far more sweeping than a few Thanksgiving turkeys and Easter hams for the hungry. Standing as both did in the rich and powerful prophetic tradition of Amos, Isaiah, and Jeremiah, they were advocating basic economic reforms. They were advocating economic systems where the rich don't just get richer and richer and the poor get poorer and poorer and the middle classes get sucked toward the bottom again.

The grinding, wrenching poverty of the huge mass of humanity which overshadows the opulent splendor of the elitist few of Rio de Janeiro will someday erupt in violence and revolution unless basic reforms take place. The grinding, wrenching poverty of the seething huddled masses yearning to breathe free will continue to yield violence and bloodshed and warfare all over the world.

Whether it is the poor of Northern Ireland, or the poor of Chiapas, Mexico, or the poor of India, or the poor Palestinians shoved into overcrowded refugee camps, or the poor of East Harlem, the prophets forever speak for those who crave a place in the sun to call their own — a place where they can work with dignity and enjoy the fruits of their labors without harassment and exploitation.

And those of us who are rich and well-off and privileged don't like the sound of the prophetic words. And those of us in unions who rightly worry about our jobs with the new trade and tariff treaties don't like it. And those of us threatened with layoffs in our corporations because of downsizing or because of corporate moves to less developed but more economic countries don't like it.

But like it or not, these prophets get under our skin because they have a universal mission and an all-encompassing compassion which reaches beyond our ethnic group or business or union or nation. They know that in the long run economic reform must take place to enable the masses of poverty-stricken peoples of the world to share in the earth's fabulous wealth. There will never be peace on earth without it. There is more than enough wealth for everyone. The prophets get under our skin, challenging us, especially our business leaders, to find ways to share in earning it, working for it, and enjoying it before it is too late.

III

Another reason prophets get under our skin is because they ask the **government not to extort with taxes.**

Under our skin, did you say? Hardly! Who could disagree with the prophets on this one? we might ask. Even if we didn't vote for Reagan a few years ago, we might have secretly resonated with his campaign promise to "get the government off our backs and out of our pockets." And most of us would agree with Justice Holmes, who said, "The power to tax is the power to kill." With the end of the year at hand, and April 15 not far behind, and with many of us paying thirty to forty percent of our income in taxes, we surely could cheer the prophets when they tell the I.R.S. not to extort through taxes.

And possibly those cheering the loudest would be those multi-millionaires *Forbes* magazine calls "The New Refugees." In a recent article (Nov. 21, 1994, p. 131), *Forbes* says that quite a number of rich Americans are renouncing their U.S. citizenship to live in places like the Bahamas and Bermuda where they are not taxed to death.

Francis Mirabello, a Philadelphia lawyer, spoke in Bermuda this fall at a conference regarding offshore money. He said, "I talk to a new client interested in expatriating every week. Many people can't pay the federal tax rate and live in the style they want." Some believe that what Judge Learned Hand called "enforced exactions" have come to be virtual confiscations, especially when it comes to estate taxes up to fifty to sixty percent. And, say *Forbes* authors Robert Lenzner and Phillippe Mao, "The exodus may speed up under an administration that campaigned for office on a tax-the-rich platform."

Their actions may sound, well, unpatriotic, but any political system which overtaxes the productive to redistribute to the nonproductive may be heading for trouble. And any government which demeans incentive and creativity by excessive and burdensome taxation may be doomed to failure. Prophets have always been criticizing governments for exploitation. And they have been getting under the skin of the citizenship as well for high expectations of eternal entitlements. Yes, there may be only two certainties in life — death and taxes. But too much of the latter by extortion will surely hasten the former.

IV

Lastly, the prophets get under our skin **because they tell us not to depend too much on military might.**

This may sound like strange advice to a nation like ours, the world's only surviving superpower. Many would say the only reason we survived is due to superior military strength. World Wars I and II are testimonies of that. So is the Korean conflict, more or less. And of course, Vietnam is still up for grabs. Nonetheless, many militarists would claim the defense buildup under Reagan helped topple the Soviet Union and bring to an end the Cold War. Could be.

But look outside our borders to a nation like Iraq and a brutal madman like Saddam Hussein. He expends huge proportions of his gross national product on arms. He is enormously in debt for his military acquisitions. He expends the lives of his citizens as cavalierly as some would expend fleas. His own men and youth mean no more to him than expendable cannon fodder. And they either have to shoot at Hussein's enemies or his commanders will shoot them in the back.

Or consider the warlords of Somalia, or the tinhorn dictators of Rwanda or Ethiopia who bring their countries to ruin. Or think of Haiti and its struggle to get out from under military rule, or the Soviet Union, which hastened its collapse due in part to over-expenditure on the military, or our own enormous national debt, fueled in part by Lyndon Johnson's "guns and butter" policy during Vietnam and Ronald Reagan's lower taxes but increased military expenditures.

Over and over again the prophets warn against putting too much trust in military might, in investing too much confidence in national military muscle. In God's eyes, says Isaiah,

> *The nations are like a drop*
>   *from a bucket*
> *and are accounted as the*
>   *dust on scales....*
> *All the nations are as nothing*
>   *before him.*
> *They are accounted by him as*
>   *less than nothing and emptiness.*
>   — 40:15, 17

Nations come and go, political leaders rise and fall, generals have their day in the sun and fade away, but the kingdom of God remains forever, says John and all the prophets. Therefore, soldiers individually and collectively should never be deceived into thinking might makes right, and that the strong are never wrong.

The problem is, say the prophets, the strong often *are* wrong, and the mighty often *are* mistaken, especially in many underdeveloped countries, not to mention Naziism and Fascism. That's why prophets get under our skin. Because just when we're resting confidently behind the massiveness of our aircraft carriers and the accuracy of our missiles and bombs and the effectiveness of our military technology — just when we were heaving a sigh of relief over the power of the military, the prophets got under our skin to point us toward the power of God and the potential corruption and perversion of the military.

Prophets — we revere them, respect them, ignore them, listen to them, and sometimes heed them. But we rarely love them — until later — because they always get under our skin. And it is usually later when we realize they needed to, had to, for our own sakes, and for God's.

Prayer

Eternal God, who in your majesty encompasses the universe and all dimensions of time and space, and who in your humility infuses all living things with the pulse of your life, as flowers and trees are inclined toward the sun's life-giving light, so are we, in our reverent worship, inclined toward you, light of all life.

In your radiant presence we always are conscious of our clouded conscience, the dimness of our insight and intelligence, aware of our faltering, flickering witness and our susceptibility to contrary winds of doubt and skepticism against our flames of faith. Forgive also our negative thinking and dour moods in the presence of so much grace and glory. Save us from any descent into the slough of despondence and rescue us from the fatal grasp of the dread. Be pleased to cleanse our souls of all unrighteousness. Make us radiant in faith and hope and love.

Speak to us anew today the truth about ourselves we have not wanted to hear. You know well those dimensions of our personality where insight has been ignored and where growth has been inhibited. Too often content with petty conceits, and too frequently circumscribed by a provincial mind-set, we fail to explore the vast spiritual and intellectual world which only awaits our energy and courage. By your grace, take us by the hand, O Lord, and lure us beyond the boundaries of our smug conceits and ready rationalizations.

But now we lift up our prayers for all the Church and world. In every place and in every day, your people struggle to keep the faith, to work for justice and peace. Give them strength. Bless your worldwide Church.

And for nations large and small, for leaders in politics, business, and the military, for diplomats and workers of every kind, we pray progress toward a greater share of wealth and freedom and opportunity for all. Help us, O God, to strive ever onward toward your glorious Kingdom envisioned by the prophets and by our Lord Jesus Christ, in whose name we pray. Amen.

Chapter 3

Someone Greater Than A Prophet

"And he will reign over the house of Jacob for ever; and of his kingdom, there will be no end."
— Luke 1:33

As our world gets smaller and smaller we become more and more aware of other cultures and religions, and we increasingly wonder about our own religion. If once we thought of them in rather exclusivistic terms, can we do so in a world which seems to have relativized exclusivistic truth claims? If once we thought of Christianity as the final word in religion, can we do so in face of a vital and resurgent Islam in the world?

In his recent, brilliant discussion of Islam, Dr. Charles Ryerson of Princeton reminded us that Moslems claim Abraham as their spiritual progenitor as do Jews and Christians. They share a common belief in one God, albeit by the name of Allah, and affirm many of the same moral values and ethical commands.

But then Dr. Ryerson went on to the central question. What do Moslems, who comprise about one sixth of the world's population, think about Jesus? Then in an answer familiar to some, but surprising to most, he asserted that Jesus is very much accepted by Islam. Not only is he respected as one of the great prophets, he is revered as a *rasul*, which means as a model man or paradigm. Not only that, Islam affirms the Virgin Birth of Jesus, which is more than many Christians will do.

But there you have it — one of the world's leading, fastest growing, resurgent religions — Islam — affirming Jesus as something greater than a prophet, as someone more than a mouthpiece and messenger for God. He is, as it were, a model man, an exemplary man, a paradigm for future generations.

That is close to what the angel Gabriel told Mary in the annunciation. He is not to be just a prophet of God. Instead, said Gabriel,

"He will be great, and will be called the son of the Most High ... and of his kingdom there will be no end" (Luke 1:32-33).

"How will I know this?" Mary asks.

"The power of the Most High will overshadow you; therefore the child to be born will be called holy, the Son of God," said Gabriel (Luke 1:35).

Yes, he is to be something more than a prophet. He is to be called the Son of God, not even just the model or the paradigm or *rasul*, but the very Son — the only begotten Son of the Father, begotten, not made, as the creed puts it.

John the Baptist, great prophet that he was, knew that the title "Son" did not belong to him. I am not the Christ, he told his followers when they asked in hopeful anticipation; I am the voice crying in the wilderness, "Prepare the way of the Lord." The One who comes after me is greater than me, greater than the prophets. I am not even worthy to untie his sandal, so great is he in comparison to me and all the prophets.

And why, John, is he greater than you and all the prophets? Because he will baptize you with the Holy Spirit and fire, and with his winnowing fork he will bring judgment between good and evil, between wheat and chaff. He is greater than the prophets.

I

Consider first the **baptism of fire**. Jesus is greater than a prophet because he brings the baptism of fire.

Fire has a variety of images in the Bible. It can mean consumption of an item in flames and thereby its reduction to gases and ashes. It can mean purgation, the burning away of impurities, as in gold refined by fire. And it can mean suffering, the fiery trials and persecutions and ordeals which many experience.

Let us consider the greatness of the Jesus who purifies by fire, who cleanses the soul of its dross by his incisive critique of our pride and pretensions. Let us envision the divine Son, who knowing firsthand what the Heavenly Father's will is, challenges all our flickering loyalties and fading allegiances to his bigger cause. But let us also behold a Christ who burns through many of the popular images constructed out of our needs and imaginations.

In his excellent book, *The Challenge of Jesus*, John Shea gives clever insight into the popular images of Christ. In answer to Jesus' famous question, "Who do you say that I am?" we have had the Jesus of Protestant piety, a blond, blue-eyed, haloed, radiant gentle-teacher; we have lost the Christ of Catholic piety, long-faced with sorrow and crowned with thorns.

In the movie, *Jesus Christ Superstar*, Jesus, says Shea, "draws the painful breaths of an existentialist anti-hero." In *Godspell* he is almost the opposite; a flower-child, a man without guile. In Ernest Renan's classic book, *The Life of Jesus*, he is a nineteenth century idealized romantic who falls on bad days. Marriage and the bourgeois life in place of revolution constitute Jesus' last temptation according to Nikos Kazantzakis' novel and movie. Of course, Marxists of liberation theology like to see Jesus as the leader of the proletarian revolt toward a classless society.

The images of Christ continue. As the pre-existent Son of God, he is the heavenly visitor, the God who comes to dinner but who exits just before the going gets tough. Radicals and revolutionaries picture him as a zealot who has come not to bring peace, but a sword. But to others he is the prototypical pacifist who advises us always to turn the other cheek.

In his book, *The Passover Plot*, Hugh Schonfield has Jesus staging his own crucifixion, intending to escape, but killed by the unexpected spear-thrust of the Roman soldier. Harvard's Harvey Cox has Jesus as a clown, as a kind of court jester amid the world's pretensions of power and position. Richard Bach, in his best-selling book, *Jonathan Livingston Seagull*, would have us believe, says Shea, that Jesus "grunted his way to divinity, the little seagull that could."

And most every cause and movement wants to quote Jesus as an authority for whatever it is they are advocating. "Jesus brings instant authority and a sense of moral imperative," says Shea. If Jesus is for it, who can be against it? And most of these people and groups do not mean to ridicule Jesus, says Shea. Instead, "each and every Jesus (they wrote) is an attempt to portray the authentic man according to a certain mission of life" (p. 23). For them Jesus becomes Jung's "ideal of the self: the 'inkblot in which each person sees what he considers true manhood (personhood)' " (p. 23).

While these multiple images are prone to manipulation and propaganda, they are, nonetheless, signs of vitality. As Shea puts it, "Jesus lives out of a transcendence which first reduces humankind to wondering silence and then to a riot of metaphors ... The many Jesuses are personal and collective searches for a cause to be committed to, a passion to be consumed by, a life which has worth and purpose" (p. 25).

And yet, Jesus is more than a prophet, because through the pages of the New Testament he brings a purifying fire which purges our self-serving, self-constructed Jesuses to see the real Jesus of power and authority who would shape us into his image of who we should be, rather than our shaping him into our image of who we want him to be for our convenience.

When we don't really know his name, "anybody can call him anything," says Shea. But Gabriel and John and Mary saw him as anything but a curiosity piece and legitimizing authority for our pet causes, however noble. He was the very Son of God. Let all other inadequate images be purged in the refining fire.

II

If John affirmed Jesus would baptize with purgative fire, he also asserted Jesus would **baptize with the Holy Spirit**.

From the beginning of the Bible to the end, the Spirit or the Holy Spirit suggests the manifestation of God's presence and power. In Genesis, at the beginning of time, we are told that "darkness was upon the face of the deep; and the Spirit of God was moving over the face of the water." In the middle of the Bible, prophets and apostles are inspired by the Holy Spirit of God, and at the end of the Bible, at the very end of all history, John the Revelator says, "The Spirit and the Bride say, 'Come.' And let him who hears say, 'Come.' And let him who is thirsty come, let him who desires take the water of life without price" (Revelation 22:17).

There it is from beginning to end, the Biblical idea of the Spirit of God as power and presence and refreshment. And it was precisely this Spirit of power and presence and refreshment which was at work in Jesus. And it was this same Spirit which he transmitted to his disciples, promising they would do even greater works in his name by the power of his Spirit.

And it was this same Spirit which inaugurated the Church on Pentecost in Jerusalem in 30 A.D., and this same Spirit which has inspired music, art, and literature, built cathedrals, orphanages, and hospitals, and nursing homes, colleges and universities; this same Spirit which has caused the Church to grow to more than a billion strong, this same creative, surging, empowering Spirit which floods minds and hearts everywhere when they are open to its presence.

Prophets are needed in every age — prophets to cut through the propaganda and rhetoric; prophets to expose the deceit and hypocrisy; prophets to deflate pompous egos and to humble arrogant hearts and minds. We need prophets to tell it like it is when everyone in little sound bites tries to convince us it is as they promise it will be. When we have been lied to, deceived, defrauded, betrayed, and suckered into one scheme after another, prophets are a breath of fresh air, a clean windshield on the future. Thank God for prophets. And thank God for John the Baptist.

But in Jesus we have someone greater than a prophet, because he not only cleanses us of corruption, but revitalizes us for a new future and empowers us for a new way of life. As theologian Daniel Williams puts it, "In Jesus Christ, God has given what is needed to heal the disorders of the human spirit, and to inaugurate a new possibility for every life" (*The Spirit and the Forms of Love*, p. 155).

Paul put it well when he said, "The first man, Adam, became a living being, the last Adam (meaning Christ) became a life-giving Spirit" (1 Corinthians 15:45). And that is what millions upon millions of people experience — the life-giving Spirit of the resurrected Christ. He empowers them with his presence to become new persons, a new creation, a new humanity. Because he is the Son, and not just a prophet, he empowers us with the creative Spirit and energy of the Father himself. Because he is greater than a prophet, we are baptized by and with his Spirit, the very Spirit of God.

III

Lastly, Jesus is more than a prophet because **he separates the wheat from the chaff**, which is to say, **he brings judgment to the world**.

Prophets brought plenty of that, of course. They thundered forth for centuries about God's justice and judgment. They faithfully warned of impending doom if repentance was not enacted. And John the Baptist, lonely, but powerful, on the bank of the Jordan River, thundered it. "Repent, for the kingdom of God is at hand."

The difference with Jesus was that he affirmed the kingdom was not only coming, it is here, present, and powerful in our very presence, and as a consequence we can be assured the wheat will be separated from the chaff — an assurance the prophets could not always give.

And when you think of it, we should be grateful for the reality of judgment. Judgment is God's way of saying, "I care about the world." Judgment means that things do matter, that there are order and coherence in place of disorder and chaos. Judgment is the confidence that eventually evil and good will be named and separated, that the righteous life does have meaning in the face of evil, that the caring person is in the end not subject to the mockery and ridicule of the uncaring.

Judgment is the affirmation of a moral universe where the distinction between right and wrong does prevail, where sense prevails over nonsense, and where meaning triumphs over absurdity. Judgment is a constant critique of the ever-prevalent mood of "anything goes" and "if it feels good, do it."

Judgment reassures us that God is more than a benign grandfather grinning like a cheshire cat with Alzheimer's at all the world's tawdriness, vanity, and hypocrisy. Judgment is the bitter end knot in the anchor rope of the universe, where finally everything is stopped and called into accountability, to give answer for all the deeds in life, good and bad, and to stand naked and undisguised without makeup before the presence of Almighty God.

Yes, he is more than a prophet because he assures us when we are choking on the chaff of life that there is indeed wheat, and that it is the bread of life. Yes, he is more than a prophet, because when we have drunk heavily the potent portions of the world's salty flotsams, he assures us there is the fresh water, the living water, from which drinking we shall never thirst again.

But most of all, he is greater than a prophet because he convicts us of our sin not so much by pushing our guilt in our face as by offering his free grace to our aching and hungry hearts.

And what he asks of us in this season and every season is a change of mind and heart, a turning away from all the trivial faiths and limited causes to which we give ultimate allegiances. By his grace, he would lure us away from all the alluring fads and entrancing idols. He would release us from our obsession with celebrities and our fascination with evil.

Is he a prophet, Dr. Ryerson? Oh yes, in the eyes of one of the great monotheistic faiths, Islam, he is greater than a prophet. He is a *rasul*, a model man, a paradigm. But in the eyes of the faithful devoted to him, in the works of the New Testament, he is even more than that. He is the very Son of God, by whom and through whom we have new life and life everlasting. And his kingdom shall never come to an end.

Prayer

Almighty God, Father of our Lord Jesus Christ and our Father, who calls the stars by name and notices when a sparrow falls, we praise and adore you for your mind which encompasses and sustains the universe, and for your heart which loves each one of us as though there were only one to love. Lovingly and ingeniously you have shaped us in your image. Patiently and tenderly you have led us by the hand over our many years of growth and development. We give you thanks.

In the rush of this season and the pressure of presents yet to buy and wrap and send, we gather here to catch our breath, to inhale deeply your refreshing Spirit into the depths of our souls. In a time when the pace is frenetic and expectations ever greater and greater, we would come into the presence of the Christ child and his waiting cross to gain a perspective on the things that matter most. For a few moments then, release us from the tyranny of schedules and the pressure of bottom lines to gain new strength and inspiration in your presence.

In this season of peace on earth and good will to men, let peace descend within our families and relationships. Replace our fears with courage. Quiet our anxieties with renewed hope. Defeat our defensiveness with a new willingness to love, even to be vulnerable. Grant that the demons of both terror and tyranny might be exorcised from our spirits so that we might be at one with you and one another and know the peace that passes all understanding.

Look with favor and compassion upon our strife-torn world. Bring new openness to the fractious parties in the former Yugoslavia, that a just peace might be negotiated. Let the ancient hostilities of the Near East subside into peaceful co-existence. Grant a just peace in Russia, in Northern Ireland, in Somalia, in the many troubled spots of our sometimes hostile world. Grant, O Lord, that we might make mighty advances toward a better life for all.

And grant your blessing of power and peaceful strength to your Church here and throughout the world, that more and more people shall come to know you through your beloved Son in whose name we pray. Amen.

Chapter 4

The Long Loneliness

Besides this you know what hour it is, how it is full time now for you to wake from sleep. For salvation is nearer to us now than when we first believed; the night is far gone, the day is at hand. — Romans 13:11-12

The Beatles surprised the world in the 1960s and took the United States by storm, introducing a new era in popular music. And many of us were pleasantly surprised by the deep insights expressed in rather direct and poignant lyrics.

In "Eleanor Rigby," for example, they sing of a woman picking up rice at a church where a wedding has been. Holding the rice, peering through a window, living in a dream she someday will wed, death comes instead. As she lived alone, so she died alone. And so the Beatles lament,

All the lonely people,
where do they all come from?

So sang the Beatles in the '60s. And so they sang again in the television Beatles' Anthology, reminding us of how they expressed a mood, introduced a revolution, and shaped an era.

With almost simple innocence the Beatles expressed a universal mood of the centuries. They tapped into a mood deeper than a lonely spinster waiting and waiting for a Prince Charming who never came to rescue her from a childless life and lonely grave. With an easy melody they expressed a melancholy deeper than that of a preacher writing a sermon which few came to hear.

All the lonely people,
where do they all come from?

"There is nothing more alone in the universe than man," says anthropologist and humanist Loren Eiseley. "He has entered into the strange world of history, of social and intellectual change, while his brothers of the field and forest remain subject to the invisible laws of biological evolution ... Man, by contrast, is alone with the knowledge of his history until the day of his death" (*The Star Thrower*, p. 37).

So it is, Eiseley would suggest, that we have been thrust out of the self-contained and self-imprisoning worlds of impulse and instinct into the worlds of thought and self-transcendence. We are *of* the world — out of the dust and minerals of the earth — earth to earth, ashes to ashes, dust to dust. And yet we are *not* of the world — we are a mind reflective and a spirit roving and free, and a heart looking and longing, like Eleanor Rigby, for fulfillment in another heart. We are mind and spirit seeking earnest responses in other minds and spirits like Reverend McKenzie, who preached a sermon for no one who came.

If after the aeons of geologic time we humans become godlike in our dominion over the other evolutionary creatures, within the confines of historic time we have that longing for something more, that deep inward sense that we are destined for another world, that innate hunger for a reality that cannot be satisfied by sensual experience alone. It will not do for us to sum up human history as did one ancient sage who said bluntly of humans: "They were born; they were wretched; they died."

If after the long, creative evolutionary process we humans popped up into the realms of self-transcendence and history-making, we have subsequently sensed the need for an overarching meaning, an underlying purpose, and an interior empowerment. However, there have been those times when we have wanted to say with poet A. E. Housman:

>   *And how am I to face the odds*
>   *Of man's bedevilment and God's?*
>   *I, a stranger and afraid*
>   *In a world I never made.*

The answer to the long loneliness of "strangers afraid in a world they never made" is to be found in Advent, in the coming of God into human history. If humans are the crowning glory of the universe's evolutionary birth process, the Bible tells us again and again that we have been emerging not into an infinite, silent void, but into the ethereal mind and spirit world of the Creator himself. The long loneliness comes to an end within time and beyond time.

- I

Let's consider first **the matter of ending the long loneliness within time.**

Probably one of the most persistently nagging questions of human existence is: "Is anyone out there? Does anyone care?" Ancient humans built their altars on mountaintops in an effort to get close to the gods up there, just beyond the solid arch of heaven, behind the blue firmament. The Tower of Babel was only one of the ziggurats pyramiding above the desert sky to probe the domain of the deities. If the gods wouldn't come down to us, we would climb up to them, because we were tired of this long loneliness of the human race. We longed for divine companionship.

In more recent times, expressing an almost equal naiveté, the early Russian cosmonauts announced to a curious and waiting world that there were no gods up there in the space orbit. There was only emptiness and the infinite reaches of space. Were we alone after all?

Not so, said the prophets of old. You cosmonauts are looking in the wrong place. You should look to history — to historical events and people. Isaiah reminded his fellow Judean exiles in Babylonia that the very God who created the brilliant stars and named them also created the Judeans as a people. God had come to them. They did not have to "climb up" to heaven to secure the companionship of God. If God talked with Adam and Eve and covenanted with Noah and Abraham, he also wrestled with Jacob and blessed him and then gave his sacred law to Moses on Mount Sinai. The God of Abraham, Isaac, and Jacob is the very God who knows all the stars by name. How then could he forget you? asks the prophet Isaiah.

The long loneliness of the Judean exiles was ended in their liberation from captivity when Cyrus allowed them to return to their homeland. God came to them in an international event through a Persian, of all people, someone whom they did not know, someone not their own, who became for them the sign of God's presence and signalled an end to their forsakeneness and sense of abandonment.

God, say the prophets, is interested in people, in their history, and in historical events. And God is not too particular whom he works through, whether it be the enemy Pharaoh or Nebuchadnezzar or Cyrus, or whether it be through Moses or David or even Yasir Arafat or Itzhak Rabin. Could not God be working through Warren Christopher and Richard Holbrooke in negotiating the Bosnian peace accord, or through President Bill Clinton endorsing and encouraging peace in Northern Ireland?

Does God leave us alone and afraid in a world we never made at the end of a long, evolutionary spiral? No, we are not abandoned into a cold, rational void of senseless and self-transcendent wondering. Not that, says the Bible in this Advent season.

Instead, we have at an intersection of the long human process a new man, a new Adam, a new model human being, who, like us, has come out of the mind and heart of God to be with us, to comfort us, and to assure us we are not alone in the world. "Don't be afraid," he tells us, "I have overcome the world" — overcome the world with its powers of loneliness and dread and despair. "And I am with you always."

II

If Advent tells us God overcomes the long loneliness **within** time, its message assures us **God intends to overcome the long loneliness beyond time.** As Paul puts it: "Salvation is nearer to us now than when we first believed: the night is far gone, the day is at hand" (Romans 13:11-12).

No doubt many of us would tend to agree with Shakespeare's Macbeth when he declares: "(Life) is a tale told by an idiot, full of sound and fury signifying nothing" (*Macbeth, V, iv.* 19). And again where he says: "All the world's a stage, and all the men and women merely players." So Shakespeare tells us in *As You Like It (II, vii, 139)*. We go through our seven roles from infant, to schoolboy, to lover, to soldier, to magistrate, to elder statesman, to drooping, dawdling second childhood, and then to death.

And Hamlet wonders for all of us: "To be, or not to be: that is the question...."

But then he muses:

> *... To grunt and sweat under a weary life,*
> *But that the dread of something after death,*
> *The undiscover'd country from whose bourn*
> *No traveler returns, puzzles the will,*
> *And makes us rather bear those ills we have*
> *Than fly to others we know not of?*
> —*Hamlet, III, i.* 56, 77-83

Is Shakespeare correct in this pessimism? Is the biblical writer of Ecclesiastes correct when he affirms that all is vanity, a chasing after the wind? Is everything futility, a brief, vaporous existence at the top of the evolutionary spiral, only to evaporate into the eternal silences of the infinite void?

Not so, says Paul in his letter to the Roman Christians. The whole universe has been groaning in travail, as if pregnant, ready to give birth to a new age. The long evolutionary process ends not with a whimper or a sigh or a bang, but with the triumph of the sons and daughters of God who are brought into glorious reunion not only with those loved long since and lost a while, but with the very Origin of their beings, with God himself.

A physical and historical and materialistic and temporal interpretation will not quite give us all the answers we need. We need to look to the spiritual aspirations of humanity and then affirm with the prophets and with the early Christians that we are dealing with a God who confronts us personally within history and assures us of life and communion and fellowship beyond history. "There's a divinity that shapes our ends, rough-hew them how we will," says Shakespeare, in a more helpful mood (*Hamlet, V, ii.* 10).

Are we alone and afraid in a world we never made? Not so, says the Bible. Not only has the Christ of God come to us, he has also given us his Spirit to empower us and to encourage us toward the end of time and beyond time. Through the Spirit we come to know God person to person, as it were. Through the agency of the Spirit, God is at work in each of our lives as an artist at work on a fresh canvas. We are a vital part of that far-off divine event toward which the whole creation moves.

If our life is a grand work of art or a gigantic symphony, it will come to climax in the Second Coming, the Second Advent of the Christ. Just as the First Advent gave us assurance and hope, so the promise of the Second Advent should infuse us with confidence and a sense of purpose.

True, as we get older we do have a tendency to "collapse into our genes," into our genetic stream, and to gain a "furniture figure" where our chest drops into our drawers! Or as we lose hope and succumb to despair we resort to the age-old nostrums of sensual stimulations, such as drunkenness or drugs or adulteries. Reveling and debauchery or the accumulation of riches and fame through ruthless greed will do little to help.

But the Church will, for we are the community of faith and hope and love where God reaches out to touch his people. And poets will help, as will musicians and artists, authors and thinkers who speak to us personally as though it was God's word, person to person. And worship will help, and prayer and study and ethics and Communion. For communion is the feast of expectation, the communal meal between the already and not yet, the holy banquet of friendliness suspended between earth and heaven, between time and beyond time. It reminds me of Salvadore Dali's painting *Christ of St. John of the Cross*, suspended as a sacrifice between heaven and earth, in time and beyond time. So it is that Communion is the foretaste of the heavenly banquet of the Lamb of God. It is the triumphant end of the long loneliness.

Prayer

Almighty God, heavenly Father, who holds the far reaches of whatever universes there may be within the power of your Being, and whose presence encompasses all the void of infinite space and time beyond time, we adore and worship you. By your exalted majesty you call us out of our small selves to tremble in your holy presence, and by your tender mercies, you draw us to yourself as children to a wise and loving father.

How can we but stand in awe of your power, and how can we but come to you as lovers as your soul speaks to our soul, more deeply than we speak to ourselves? We thank you.

Yet it is for us to confess that we are often blinded to your glory by trivial concerns and we frequently become indifferent to your mercy within a brutal and violent world. Save us, O God, from succumbing to the age-old numbness which makes us insensitive to you. And break up these calcified hearts and arthritic souls, that we might be open and vital with your Mind and Spirit.

In this Advent season we lift up before you all the lonely people of the world. We think of mothers bereft of sons and wives bereft of husbands in the Bosnian-Serb conflict. We call to mind little girls in Northern Ireland who have known the grief of fathers murdered before their very eyes, and we bring before you the anguish of little Palestinian and Israeli boys whose fathers or brothers lie silent in the tomb. And for the victims of violent crime in this country, their parents and spouses, children and loved ones, who know the long days of grief and the endless nights of tears — for these, O God, and thousands more, we pray your healing balm of Gilead.

But perhaps closer at hand and nearer to our own selves we bring before you the loneliness of our own hearts — the soul seeking the soulmate, the widow left fibrillating alone without her defining partner, the divorcée struggling with regret, relief, and a new hope for a new and fulfilling future, the child who has never felt understood, so alone, and tempted toward alcohol or drugs for solace, the couple in a tired marriage where neither is really there for the other, the unemployed rejected now and again in the search for affirmation and gain, the persons of the almost and not-quite-yet who wonder if they ever will fulfill their dreams — for all these and more, O God, we make our supplications to you. In your divine wisdom and mercy, be pleased to grant our requests.

And thank you, God — thank you for a many-splendored world, the miraculous and marvelous in all living things, and for the Christ who speaks to us of your very mind and heart. We praise you in his name. Amen.

Chapter 5

A Voice To Be Heard

"I am the voice of one crying in the wilderness, 'Make straight the way of the Lord....'" — John 1:23

It had been a long time. History seemed more moribund and leaden than ever. Hope was either frozen or fanatic. Cynicism was the daily fare and optimism the dream of fools. So it was in those days of long ago.

But now there was a stirring in history's corridors — not in the throne rooms of Rome or Alexandria, not in the libraries of Athens or the armies of Caesar — but in little backwater towns of a troublesome, rebellious, backwater country.

The first of the stirrings began in Jerusalem with a tired old priest, childless and lonely in his old age, enduring the oppression of his time with his barren wife Elizabeth. While attending to his priestly duties of burning incense at the Temple altar, the old priest Zechariah had a startling vision. The archangel Gabriel appeared to him and said, "Your prayer has been heard. Your wife Elizabeth will bear a son, and you shall name him John ... He will be great in the eyes of the Lord ... He will go before the Lord as a forerunner, possessed by the spirit and power of Elijah ... to prepare a people fit for the Lord" (Luke 1:13-17).

This was no vague hope, no wild dream of an old man who should know better. What he saw actually came to pass, and those preliminary stirrings began to shake the foundations of history.

And as the child, John, grew up, he became strong in spirit and began living in the wilderness. In a life of solitude, of prayer and fasting, he sensed he was not alone, that the New Age of God's Messiah was at hand. History's long-awaited day was coming. The Christ was approaching. The time of God's anointed was near.

The wilderness silence could contain John no longer. He felt the impulses of the ages in his soul. His veins throbbed with the zeal of God. Blowing through his hair and beard and very soul was the wind of the hills, God's Wind, God's Spirit. The fire of judgment belched from his nostrils. His eyes were aflame with righteousness, his heart thrusting the lifeblood of hope and expectancy through his being. He had to preach. He was compelled to speak out.

> *Prepare the way of the Lord,*
> *make straight in the desert*
> *a highway for our God.*
> *The kingdom of heaven is at hand.*
> *Prepare the way of the Lord.*

Sure he was fiery and uncompromising, nearly a radical, a fanatic. But the sins of the people were oppressive and deadening. The structures of life were drawn tight and everyone was suffocating. John burst the bonds and began to set the captives free — free from their sins, free from their smothering compromises, free from their lack of vision and hope and imagination.

No wonder Jesus, in admiration, remarked: "What did you go out in the wilderness to see? A reed shaken by the wind? Why then did you go out? To see a prophet? Yes, I tell you, and more than a prophet" (Matthew 11:7-9).

Even though the official deputation of priests, Levites, and Pharisees didn't want to admit it, they were hearing a prophet. He called them a den of snakes. King Herod, against his better judgment, came out to listen to the wilderness preacher, and he knew he had heard a prophet because he heard the truth about himself — a truth all his palace yes-men would never speak.

And ever since those days of long ago, we have been gathering again and again to hear the Baptist's cry. Speaking over nineteen centuries ago, his voice resounds across history to this very moment, to this very place. In his time, Tiberius Caesar was issuing official proclamations to be spread throughout the world by official couriers of power and authority.

But John — the lonely, uncompromised John of the wilderness — shouted from the hillside, and his voice is still the voice that should be heard and is heard, this very day, by thousands of couriers in thousands of churches announcing the Lord's Advent. "Who are you, John?" they asked. "I am the voice of one crying in the wilderness, 'Make straight the way of the Lord.' " He is the voice to be heard.

I

John's voice was heard because he had **the courage to speak out.** He spoke out bravely, courageously, daringly, in ways that eventually cost him his life.

There were a thousand priests mumbling the words of the Lord in the seclusion of their sanctuaries day after day. Service after service Levites sung and chanted the message of God. Lawyers, by the thousands, studied the law every day and knew it by heart. Yet in public they all said what everyone wanted to hear. Only in private did they whisper the truth.

But not John. He stood up and spoke out. He had no real credentials. He was without backing from any official group. No newspaper or television station or church or college stood behind him. He had no degrees, no best-selling books, and had appeared on no talk shows. He was not a member of a powerful family. He was without independent resources and existed on food from the wilderness. Uncompromised, he cried aloud, he spoke out, he proclaimed the truth.

It occurs to me that our age is not unlike John's. Instead of the Romans oppressing us, it often is our own government. The Caesars do not threaten us. Instead we are intimidated by our bureaucracies. Witness, for example, the frequent destruction of personal property by narcotics authorities.

In one city, a narc squadron of government authorities invaded a citizen's house, suspecting drugs were hidden there. They overturned every piece of furniture, knocked holes in walls, displaced clothing, tore apart pictures, only to discover they had chosen the wrong house. The last I knew, the people had not been adequately compensated by the government.

Or consider the example of narcotics agents seizing a young man's new sailboat in the Caribbean, a sailboat he had just bought for $24,000 and was now enjoying on his vacation. Federal narcotics agents boarded the boat and literally destroyed it looking for drugs they never found because there were none. At last report, he had been compensated only $8,000 of the $24,000 he spent on the boat.

Not long ago the United States Surgeon General, Joycelyn Elders, suggested a terribly politically incorrect idea. She suggested that we study the possibility of decriminalizing drugs. So much crime and violence is connected to drugs, she suggested — as had George Shultz, Milton Friedman, and William F. Buckley before her — that our country would be a much safer, saner place if we legalized drugs. If we take the high price out of drugs, would we not collapse the drug cartels and the drug violence overnight?

After all, asks Robert Reno in one of his columns, is drug use really a national epidemic? About 0.9 percent of the population regularly uses cocaine. If you double that to include crack and heroin use, you still have less than two percent of the population using drugs.

But seven percent of Americans have heart problems. Nearly eleven percent have high blood pressure, twelve percent have arthritis. Smokers comprise 27 percent of our population and users of alcohol, 51 percent. Reno humorously adds that those who suffer from ingrown toenails and chronic constipation are 2.3 percent and 1.9 percent, respectively. Says Robert Reno, "Drug-related violence may seem epidemic, but clearly drug abuse isn't, when compared with most diseases" (*Newsday*, December 10, 1993, p. 64).

But think of all the billions and billions spent on drug enforcement. Think of all the violence connected with enforcement, production, and selling of drugs, and all the violence of druggies stealing and maiming to get money for their habit. Why not just give it to them under controlled conditions, and take crime and violence and mayhem and death out of drugs? Why not treat drug use and addiction like alcohol and tobacco abuse?

As it turned out, the new-breed Democrats in the White House distanced themselves from Surgeon General Elders. The drug control and drug enforcement program has been inconsequential in stemming the flow of drugs or curbing their use. Legalize drugs and we may experience a huge drop in burglaries, maimings, muggings, vandalisms, and murders. Many of us cringe at such ideas because we know we have remained silent when we should have spoken out.

Oh, John, you God-fearing, fire-spitting ascetic. You make us shudder. We are afraid to listen to you, yet we are afraid not to. You judge us like T.S. Eliot, "As the hollow men/The stuffed men." With your voice ringing in our ears we shall have to speak up for justice and righteousness and an end to tyranny and oppression. Yours is indeed a voice we hear.

II

If John's was a voice to be heard because he had the courage to speak out, his was also a voice to be heard because he had the **courage to speak in — to speak to the human heart and soul.**

If Isaiah before him had prophesied a highway through the wilderness of the Arabian desert for the Lord, John was now prophesying a way into the human soul. As noted Biblical scholar Raymond Brown puts it, John was preparing not a highway in the desert. He was preaching "opening up the hearts of men, levelling their pride, filling their emptiness, and thus preparing them for God's intervention" (*Anchor Bible*, Vol. 29, Gospel of John, p. 50).

John knew the coming of the Lord needed no freeway across the wasteland of Judean geography. John demanded a way be made for the Lord through the wasteland of Judean hearts. The world was not in need of another Roman road to Rome. It needed instead a great way from the soul to the true Eternal City. "Prepare the way of the Lord. Make his paths straight."

John knew people. He knew how crooked and devious their lives could be. He saw the deceit and self-deception. Fornicators and adulterers had all the covers lifted to be exposed to the searing light of conscience. Hypocrites and phonies, young and old, were exposed as the parasites they were on God's society. The self-righteous were blown off their pedestals by the blast of his word of truth. Idols with feet of clay crumbled in the presence of his thunderous voice.

People who had been living miserly, self-centered lives looked in the mirror and saw themselves for the first time as they really were — as Ebenezer Scrooges. Talented people burying their abilities beneath trivial activities were summoned to the stage, front and center, for performance in keeping with their gifts. In the secret reaches of bank vaults and stock portfolios, the wealthy were reminded, "Unto whom much is given, much is required." The poor were summoned from the idol of greed and envy, and reminded to seek first the Kingdom of God.

Some time ago, a young executive of the '60s generation came up to me and said, "You know, I think my generation emphasized external, societal morality while the previous generation emphasized internal, personal morality. That generation believed a moral person would produce a moral society. My generation believed a moral society would produce a moral person."

But John addressed both. If his was a voice that spoke out for social justice and structures of morality, it was also a voice which spoke inwardly for individual integrity. If it was a mistake to believe moral people automatically produce a moral society, it was also a mistake to believe a moral society will produce moral people. A good structure administered by corrupt people can produce corruption. And a good person administering a bad structure can still produce corruption.

These days we don't like John's message of personal repentance. If we have the courage, we much prefer to talk about problems out there — about political and economic reform, about accountability, efficiency, and effectiveness in our educational system, about urban renewal and social action. These should be talked about.

But John presses his message of change even further, right on into the heart of every hearer. And the message is — repent, turn around, open up, make God the center of your life instead of self, or family, or business, or profession, or sports, or success, or power, or money, or popularity, or status. Turn away from those lifeless, death-dealing idols, says John. Open up to the living God. Make a straight path to your heart for him.

Are you resistant or afraid? You have every right to be. I am afraid, for when I look into the power of God, I am afraid I may lose control, afraid he will make me into something I do not want to become, afraid he will destroy my self-image or alter it beyond my planning, afraid I will lose some friends or ruffle some feathers, afraid my religion will become unreasonable.

Afraid? Yes, we're afraid because, as T.S. Eliot put it, "Our age is an age of moderate virtue/And of moderate vice" ("The Rock"). We're afraid we'll be shaken out of our moderate mediocrity into something fearful and great. Afraid our little kingdoms of self-centeredness will be broken up, afraid our trivial concerns will be consumed in the refiner's fire, afraid our faith will snap like in the blast of the Baptist's voice.

You bet we're afraid — afraid to let go the grudges we've been nursing and hiding behind for years, afraid to confess the hatreds and hostilities we have for ministers and other church leaders, afraid to let go the defenses and excuses we've been erecting between God's church and ourselves. Yes, we're afraid of letting fresh, invigorating air into the stuffy, volatile, seething conceits of our souls, afraid God's power will put us off the throne.

And yet, John's voice is the voice to be heard to prepare the way of the Lord. It's a voice that speaks up and out and a voice that speaks down into the very depths of our souls. And it says, repent. Open up and receive the Christ anew and you and your church and society will be made whole.

Prayer

Almighty God, Creator of all things, who holds the universe in the palm of your hand, and yet who participates in its ebb and flow, out of the infinite reaches of your Being, you have brought forth your Word, giving us tongues to speak and sing and ears to hear. Loving Father, author of all silence and sound, it has pleased you to bless us with bird songs and violins, the sounds of waves against the shore and mysterious winds through the forests. Choirs and symphonies enrich our souls, and prophets and poets inspire our minds and hearts to rise above the mere mundane. Thanks and praise be to you, loving Creator of us all.

If in times past there were lack of sounds and voices, in our time we are overwhelmed with a cacophony of noise. Strident voices demand to be heard. Radical voices insist on their righteousness. Racist voices of every color strain our sense of community. Fanatic voices insist on their way. The politically correct thwart contrary opinions and public officials often obscure the voice of truth. O Eternal God, who sees beyond all appearances to penetrate to the truth, help us to hear your voice of wisdom amid all the competing voices of today.

In your presence it is for us to confess that we often have ignored your word for us. In the deep reaches of conscience you have wanted to speak to us. From the freshness of early morning insight you have nudged us toward higher goals. In late night reflection you have moved in our hearts to remind us we are yours, no matter how tenuous and fragile our lives might be.

Forgive us when we ignore you, O Lord, when we turn our attention to competing lesser voices, or when we turn off our spiritual hearing aids to indulge the passions of the moment. Grant us courage and humility to listen with openness to your voice which is the truth, the way, and the life.

Give us each, we pray, the word we need to hear. If we are discouraged, the word of hope; if we are confused, the word of clarity; if we are tempted, the word of strength; if we are ill, the word of healing; if we are stubborn, the word of faith over fear; if we are arrogant, the word of humility; if we are legalistic, the word of grace; if we are hateful and revengeful, the word of forgiveness; if we are bitter, the word of charity; if we are mournful, the word of comfort and hope.

O Eternal God, the very Word of the universe and all life, in your mercy speak to us anew the word we need in our inmost heart and soul. And help us most to rejoice in your Son, the very Word which became flesh, who came to dwell among us, full of grace and truth. May we receive that Word with all our heart and mind. Amen.

Chapter 6

The Unexpected Universe

> *"Go and tell John what you hear and see: the blind receive their sight and the lame walk, lepers are cleansed and the deaf hear, and the dead are raised up, and the poor have good news preached to them. And blessed is he who takes no offense at me."* — Matthew 11:4-6

It has already caused a stir in the minds of many. Long-held doubts have surfaced. A steady skepticism seems to be reinforced. The college cynic seems to be confirmed. And the village atheist smiles in self-congratulation.

But there it was nevertheless. *Time* magazine's cover story asking whether the Bible really can be verified from an archeological point of view. Were the patriarchs, Abraham, Isaac, and Jacob, mere legendary characters with no real, historical existence?

Was Moses pure myth, as my former seminary classmate and now eminent archeologist, William Dever, was quoted as saying? Was the famous Exodus of the Israelites from Egypt a fabrication to undergird the later Israelites with a heroic founding legend? Did the famous King David ever actually exist or was he a fabrication of later writers, the invention of historians who needed an acceptable past for their people?

There are no proofs of the existence of Abraham, Isaac, and Jacob, say many archeologists. Nor is there proof the Israelites were in Egypt. Nor is there proof of an Exodus across the Sinai Peninsula behind a mythological Moses, say other archeologists. And there is no evidence of the military conquest of Jericho by Joshua and Caleb, say other diggers into the remains of the past.

However, the absence of archeological evidence does not mean the evidence is absent, say many. Besides, one archeological discovery, such as that of the Dead Sea Scrolls in 1947, can suddenly corroborate and verify a whole period of Biblical history.

But an even more important question has to do with past and future. Does the future of religion depend on archeological corroboration? Are our expectations for the future buried in the ruins of the past? And for answer we turn to another archeologist and paleontologist of our time, Loren Eiseley, and his book from which we get our sermon title, *The Unexpected Universe*.

In the book, Eiseley tells of his unexpected visit to a city garbage dump, where one of the red-eyed dump workers said, "We get it all. Just give it time to travel, we get it all," even aborted babies. Eiseley mused as to how archeologists grub around the ruins and garbage heaps of civilizations looking for confirmation of the notion that as things are they have always been.

But that's not the way it works, says Eiseley. That's not how the natural world works. Nature is not an endless repetition of the past, but suddenly, unforetold and unexpected in geologic time, the world is surprised with the appearance of flowers or the emergence of the human brain — all unpredicted by any would-be archeologists of the time looking for evidences in the past to inhibit the future.

God does not play dice with the universe, says Eiseley, agreeing with Einstein, but there are unpredictability, novelty, mutation, and radical change in the natural world. And then it happens in the human world — in Axial Periods of human history — periods when the Second Isaiah or Buddha or Plato or Christ appear — periods when human thought and history are changed forever. "The words spoken by the carpenter of Nazareth are those of a world changer," says Eiseley. "They mark ... the rise of a new human image, a rejection of purely material goals, a turning toward some inner light" (*The Invisible Pyramid*, p. 147).

Was the dump philosopher correct — if he waits long enough, it comes to him and he will see it all? Are the archeologists correct? If they dig long enough, will they somehow see the present and future in the ruins of the past? Probably not, says Eiseley, because in the natural world we keep having emerge an unexpected universe. And in the human world too, in Axial Periods, a new and unexpected way of seeing emerges.

And so it is with our text — John the Baptist of the old world, Jesus of Nazareth of the new; John the Baptist, prophet par excellence of the old age, Jesus the Rabbi, prophet par excellence of the age to come — inaugurator of the unexpected universe.

I

Consider first the **expected universe of John the Baptist.**

Had you and I been living in those days we would have shared his expectations. John was not without hope. He was not a defeatist or pessimist. No dour cynicism and comfortable skepticism were to be found in this austere, self-denying, wilderness monk.

Quite the contrary, he was full of hope. He expected something new. The Kingdom of God was coming. He wanted to speak to the masses, to warn them, to prepare them, to baptize them, to cleanse their souls for the coming kingdom.

And talk to the masses he did — this striking figure in camel's hair coat and leather belt. Ascetic, austere, lean and almost mean from the disciplines of the severe wilderness hermit life, his booming voice penetrated the most hardened of hearts and seared the most sated of consciences.

Even King Herod came. Not Herod the Great, but his son, Herod Antipas, came out in his chariot in all his royal robes to hear the rustic preacher by the Jordan River. Any nervous king would be suspicious of John, but Herod may also have had a twinge of conscience. On a recent trip to Rome he had seduced his brother Philip's wife, came back, divorced his own wife, and married his sister-in-law. Herod was publicly excoriated for his sin by courageous, fearless John.

That's why now (in our text for today), John is in the dungeon at the Machaerus Fortress near the Dead Sea — in prison where Herod had put him, even though in his heart, Herod knew John was a prophet of God. And it is from prison John sends some of his disciples to inquire of Jesus, "Are you the one who is to come, or should we look for another?"

And who, we might ask, was John looking for? He tells us the one he was looking for was mightier, more powerful than he. He would baptize not so much with water, but with fire, the fire of judgment, and with the Spirit, the Spirit of God, just as King David was infused with the Spirit.

In fact, that's who he and thousands were expecting, a new King David, a new mighty man manifesting the irresistible power of one possessed of the Spirit of God. If King Saul had slain his thousands and King David his tens of thousands, then the Messiah, the Anointed One, the New King David would conquer his hundreds of thousands.

But it wasn't happening. Jesus hadn't even managed to muster enough power to get John out of prison. There was no word of Jesus' recruiting soldiers, no evidence of well-armed volunteers receiving training on weekends, no indication of developing political-military strategies.

John's new Kingdom of God, his new universe, was an expected universe. It was an anticipation of a return to military might for Israel, albeit a righteous and devoted military might. It was the expected universe of the Psalms of Solomon which predicted of the coming Messiah in these words:

> *Behold, O Lord, and raise up for them*
> *their King, the Son of David ...*
> *And gird him with strength to shatter*
> *the unrighteous rulers ...*
> *And gird him with strength ...*
> *With a rod of iron to break in*
> *pieces all their resources....*
> (Chapter 17)

I remember some years ago seeing the dramatic movie *Top Gun*. Of course, some critics complained it was essentially a recruiting film for the U.S. Navy as we witnessed those "top gun" jet pilots take off from the enormous aircraft carriers, their afterburners blazing in dawn's early light, to perform unbelievable maneuvers, and then to land again with an aerial view of our massive naval power. It was very impressive. I myself was almost recruited!

But it's an old worldview. Powerful as it is, it's a vision of an expected universe of one military power supplanting another, a universe of sometimes blatant military power, a world which easily descends into might makes right; a world of revenge upon revenge upon revenge, in rituals of ethnic cleansings which vent centuries of unforgiven hatreds.

And in his own way, righteous though he was, John was looking for, hoping for, and anticipating an expected universe. So he told his disciples to ask Jesus, "Are you the one to come, or should we look for another?"

II

So now our focus turns with John and his disciples toward **Jesus and the unexpected universe**.

So, Jesus, are you the one who is to come, or should we look for another? Jesus quietly, and without anxiety, said to John's disciples, "Go and tell John what you hear and see: the blind receive their sight and the lame walk, lepers are cleansed and the deaf hear, and the dead are raised up, and the poor have good news preached to them. And blessed is he who takes no offense at me" (Matthew 11: 4-6). (And yet we still take offense at him and have difficulty really believing what he said.)

These were indeed Messianic answers taken from Isaiah chapters 35 and 61. Yes, the Messianic Age was idealized as a time when all diseases would be healed. Yes, the Messianic Age would be the occasion of the poor having the good news of shared prosperity preached to them. Yes, the Messiah would inaugurate a new era of peace and prosperity, but it was to be by the strength of a military-political leader, unparalleled since King David's time.

The other day our service club went down to the local senior center to serve them lunch, which we cater in for their holiday enjoyment. We serve the lunch, sing Christmas carols, and give them gifts. In my Prayer of Invocation I asked God for peace in the Bosnian-Serbian conflict, in Northern Ireland, in the Middle East, and in our own cities and families. After the prayer there was a loud and hearty, unanimous "Amen," almost as good as the applause I sometimes get for prayers at well-champagned wedding receptions!

As I served an older man his lunch, he said, "You know, I really appreciated your prayer for peace. A lot of people don't know what war is all about. Some of these young people have romantic notions about war. But I," he continued, "I was in World War II, and I have seen enough of blood and slaughter. It's time for a new way of doing things," he said. "War is way out of date."

"You're right," I replied. Here was an elderly man, a World War II veteran, looking for the unexpected universe, looking for something really new. I was reminded of Leon Wolff's classic book, *In Flanders Fields*, and his gripping account of the endless misery and suffering in the muck and mire of the trenches and the mustard gas warfare of World War I. What unbelievable human sacrifices were made for a few yards of sodden real estate. Is it any wonder that World War I poet, Wilford Owen, himself a soldier on the front, wrote:

> *I dreamed King Jesus fouled*
> *   the big gun gears:*
> *And caused a permanent*
> *   stoppage in all bolts;*
> *And buckled with a smile*
> *   mausers and colts;*
> *And rusted every bayonet*
> *   with his tears.*

It was that unexpected universe which Jesus was introducing when in the Garden of Gethsemane he told Peter to put away the sword, for those who live by the sword, die by the sword. It was that unexpected universe he was introducing when he wept over the city of Jerusalem for its salvation rather than ruling over it with the sword for its exploitation.

It was that unexpected universe which he was introducing when he decided to end the expected universe of the revenge to end all revenge; the victory to end all other victories; the domination to end all other dominations; and the power to place into subservience all other powers. And he did it all in his own body, in his own person, saying, I did not come to dominate and exploit, but to serve, and to give my life as a ransom for many.

Well, you might ask, is this unexpected universe in place and actually working? Are the blind seeing, the lame walking, the deaf hearing, and the poor having good news preached to them?

Yes, because for every well-publicized, Nobel Peace Prize winning Albert Schweitzer and Mother Teresa, there are thousands upon thousands upon thousands engaged in the complex work of healing. And while the innate healing process is miracle enough, there are thousands of minds and hands and hearts at work in the health and healing professions because they, more than being committed to the profit motive, are committed to Christ's unexpected universe. So our hospitals often are named St. Luke's or St. Mary's or St. Vincent's or Methodist or Presbyterian.

Is this unexpected universe in place and working, you ask? My wife and I recently attended an All-Africa dinner in Manhattan in connection with the Fiftiethth Anniversary festivities of the United Nations. One award recipient, a woman, the Executive Director of the YWCA in Uganda, had expanded her organization from a few hundred to nearly three million women, even during the time of the hideous Idi Amin. She brought health, wholeness, liberation, education, and self-respect to thousands upon thousands of women. Why? Because she is devoted to the Christ and his unexpected universe.

Is this unexpected universe in place and working, you ask? Twice we have visited Olympia in Greece where the Olympic Games began. I love the ruins there — the Temple of Apollo, the Temple of Hera, and, of course, the ancient stadium itself, where I ran a foot-race with my friends.

But not far from the stadium are the ruins of the Rotunda, erected by Alexander the Great, in which he placed statues of his family. The statues are long gone. The majestic columns of the Rotunda lie about in pieces — a crumbled monument of Alexander the Great, who, as legend says, wept because there were no more worlds to conquer.

But travel a little farther from Olympia to Sparta or Patras or Athens, or farther to Rome or Paris or London, or farther to New York or Chicago or San Francisco, or farther to Honolulu or Hong Kong or Beijing or Tokyo or Moscow or St. Petersburg — travel on and you will find them, monuments not to Alexander the Great, but monuments to King Jesus, working, living monuments, beautiful monuments, full of people with hope in their eyes, with prayers and songs on their lips and love and peace in their hearts. And they are all a part of it — the unexpected universe, the surprise of the ages, the startling awakening to a new way of life and reality, never to be found in the ruins of the past.

Jesus, "Are you the one who is to come, or should we look for another?" Oh, he is the One, and he is here with his unexpected universe.

Prayer

Almighty God, Creator of the universe and our Creator, whose nature it is always to create, and who through our telescopes grants us visions of galaxies expanding and stars being formed, and who through our microscopes takes us from infinite largeness to infinite smallness, to macrocosms and microcosms of your creative power which dazzle us with wonder and excite us with curiosity and awe, we praise you. Our finest music and noblest literature would not be adequate to praise you. And yet from these inadequate tongues and lips we utter our thanks and adoration.

As in our mind's eye and heart's imagination we present ourselves before you, we become aware of the frequent smallness of the worlds we invent for ourselves. Comfortable with familiar ideas, we never venture far from our intellectual neighborhood. Too often satisfied with the palliatives of platitudes and clichés, we avoid the unfamiliar and unknown. Fixed in the routine of set social habits and acceptable patterns of thought, we tend to conclude there is nothing new under the sun, and that as things have been, they always shall be.

O God of the universe, mind and energy of all that is and is to be, forgive us our smallness of mind and timidity of thought. Help us to remember that your thoughts are higher than our thoughts, your ways nobler than our ways, and that we should always be learning from you. Cause us to remember the pioneers in science and technology, the adventurers in the exploration of earth and space, the researchers into medicine and health, the thinkers and seers and inventors and creative people of all ages who have challenged the old, introduced the new, and have brought us into an unexpected universe. O God, be pleased to attend us with your Spirit and grace that we might continue to develop the potential that is within us all.

And now in your fatherly tenderness, hear the requests we make for those in special need — for the student bogged down by discouragement, worried that she will never achieve more than her parents; for the young man discouraged in his career because of reversals and misfortune; for the parents with a wayward child seemingly beyond reach; for the grandparents, lonely and not well and feeling neglected; for the spouses deadlocked in stalemate and boredom; for the churches so acculturated and tradition-bound that they offer no alternative light to the world; for politicians and diplomats who have forgotten they are to serve rather than exploit — for these and many more, O God, we bring our earnest requests into your presence. Be pleased to hear and answer. Through Jesus Christ our Lord. Amen.

Chapter 7

The Star Thrower

When they heard the king they went their way; and lo, the star which they had seen in the East went before them, till it came to rest over the place where the child was. When they saw the star they rejoiced exceedingly with great joy.
— Matthew 2: 9-10

O Star (the fairest one in sight),
We grant your loftiness the right
To some obscurity of cloud –
It will not do to say of night,
Since dark is what brings out your light.
Some mystery becomes the proud.
But to be wholly taciturn
In your reserve is not allowed.
Say something to us we can learn
By heart and when alone repeat.
Say something! And it says "I burn."
— Robert Frost, "Choose Something Like A Star"

The Star of Bethlehem associated with this holy season was taciturn and mysterious. It was lofty and reserved. Yet this fabled conjunction of the planets Jupiter and Saturn in 7 B.C. was thought to be saying considerably more to humanity than simply, "I burn." Stargazers of the ancient Near East watched carefully for signs from the Divine Star Thrower — astrological signs affecting terrestrial destinies.

Within Judaism, Balaam's star prophecy of many centuries earlier had been associated with the Messiah's birth, where he said:

"I see him, but not now;
I behold him, but not nigh:

> *A star shall come forth out of Jacob,*
> *and a scepter shall rise out of Israel...."*
> — Numbers 24:17

Matthew seems to attach this prophecy to the appearance of the Star of Bethlehem.

But even more intriguing are the expectations of a coming Messiah suggested by sources outside Judaism. Roman historian Suetonius, in his *Life of Vespasian*, says, "There had spread all over the Orient an old and established belief, that it was fated at that time for men coming from Judea to rule the world." Tacitus, the historian, writes, "There was a firm persuasion ... that at this very time the East was to grow powerful and rulers coming from Judea were to acquire a universal empire."

Therefore, it would not be unusual for these wise men, these Median astrologers of the priestly class of Persia (modern Iran), to note the special significance of the conjunction of Jupiter and Saturn in the desert's brilliant nighttime sky. These fascinating and intriguing ancient experts in medicine, philosophy, and astrology knew this particular heavenly sign had divine significance for Judea and for the world. The Star Thrower of the universe was using this star these nights long ago to tell us something.

And what was that? We might ask. Robert Frost has the answer when he continues about the "fairest star in sight":

> *It asks a little of us here.*
> *It asks of us a certain height,*
> *So when at times the mob is swayed*
> *To carry praise or blame too far,*
> *We may choose something like a star*
> *To stay our minds on and be staid.*

That's it: the Heavenly Star Thrower wants to stay our minds so we carry neither praise nor blame too far.

I

Consider first **the matter of praise.**

One need not look long to see humanity's age-old propensity to carry praise too far. Consider, for example, some of the titles of rulers of the past: Alexander the Great, Herod the Great, Caesar Augustus, Antiochus Epiphanes, meaning the manifestation of the Divine. Can you hear it now? Governor Pataki the Great, or President Bill Clinton, Ephiphanes!

Other rulers of history were not overwhelmed with modesty. Some of the Caesars began to demand that they be worshiped as gods. The Emperor of Japan until recent times was thought to be the representation of the Divine on earth. And in the West, as well as the East, the doctrine of the divine right of kings was well in place.

In fact, it was quite well in place with Herod the Great. He had been made King of Judea in 40 B.C. by the Roman Senate. Shrewd, capable, sometimes even magnanimous, Herod was, nevertheless, cruel and ruthless. When he suspected treason on the part of his family members, he murdered his beautiful and beloved wife Marianne and her mother Alexandra. He assassinated his sons, Alexander and Aristobulus. When Caesar Augustus heard about it in Rome he said that, in the Kosher climate of Judea, it was safer to be Herod's pigs (*hus*) than his sons (*huios*).

Herod's self-praise knew no bounds. And yet most of us know about Herod only because he rides along on the shirttails of Jesus, to whom the Heavenly Star Thrower was pointing with his Star of Bethlehem, which would have arrested the attention of Robert Frost as much as it did that of the Wise Men.

Carrying praise too far is a common problem in human history. We westerners came out of the nineteenth century patting ourselves on the back at our own proud achievements. In every way and in every day our world is getting better and better, we told ourselves with our theory of inevitable progress. The twentieth century, said some, would be the "Christian Century," the century when many of the highest Christian ideals would come to fruition.

Arrogance and optimism were high in those days. Perhaps the confident, arrogant mood is best represented in Oscar Wilde's somewhat prideful witticism when he said, "When I went to America, I had two secretaries; one for autographs, the other for locks of hair.

Within six months the one had died of writer's cramp, the other was completely bald."

Architect Frank Lloyd Wright, my fellow Wisconsin native, was not known for his modesty. As the architect of the age, he typified the arrogance. When an attorney characterized Frank Lloyd Wright as America's greatest architect, Wright confessed to his wife that he could not deny it because he was under oath!

But praise had been carried too far. World War I ensued with its massive slaughter. Then came the Great Depression, World War II and massive deaths, the Korean conflict, and the Vietnam War. That is why neo-orthodox theologians like Karl Barth, himself in the trenches in World War I, urged us to look again at the Star of Bethlehem, so as not to carry praise too far.

If we carry praise too far in political systems and ideologies, we tend also to carry it too far in the realm of science and knowledge. In the Middle Ages it was the Church which carried praise too far with respect to its cosmology, so that people like Copernicus were suspect and people like Galileo were excommunicated. How dare they suggest the earth revolved around the sun and not vice versa. The medieval Church needed to look up to the heavens again to look for signs from the Star Thrower so that its arrogance and cruelty might have been humbled.

In our own time, it is not so much the Church that is humbled, but science itself. And just now, astronomers and cosmologists are perplexed about the nature of the cosmos and the direction of the universe. Now able to see fascinating new sights through the Hubble telescope orbiting in space, astronomers are increasingly uncertain about the universe, its age, and its make-up as they watch stars being formed in the far reaches of space.

Is the universe younger than the stars it contains? It seems to be, says astronomer Wendy Freedman of the Carnegie Observatory in Pasadena, California. Is there dark matter out there? Is there an undiscovered basic particle out there? If once we thought we had it all figured out, astronomers and cosmologists now wonder if modern cosmology, the science of the cosmos, is on the verge of collapse. "If you ask me," says astrophysicist Michael Turner of the Fermi National Accelerator Laboratory near Chicago, "either we're close to a breakthrough, or we're at our wit's end" (*Time* magazine, March 6, 1995, p. 76).

But astrophysicist John Bahcall, of the Institute for Advanced Study in Princeton, says, "Every time we get slapped down, we can say, 'Thank you, Mother Nature,' because it means we're about to learn something important" (*Time*, March 6, 1995, p. 84). I think he's right. God always resists the proud, but gives wisdom and grace to the humble.

Centuries ago at this season the Heavenly Star Thrower was getting the world's attention to say with Robert Frost:

> *So when at times the mob is swayed*
> *To carry praise or blame too far,*
> *We may choose something like a star*
> *To stay our minds on and be staid.*

A star like the Star of Bethlehem, the Star of David, the Messiah, who with his humility has humbled all the Herods and Caesars and Kaisers and Kings and philosophers of the world. And he would humble us too.

II

Let us look now at **the matter of blame**.

If on the one hand the Star of Bethlehem signalled the humbling of the proud and arrogant, on the other hand it signalled the encouragement and exaltation of the humble, the poor, the downtrodden, and the outcasts. In her beautiful Magnificat, Jesus' mother, Mary, prophesied it when she sang:

> *My soul magnifies the Lord...*
> *he has put down the mighty from*
> *   their thrones,*
> *and exalted those of low degree;*
> *he has filled the hungry with good*
> *   things,*
> *and the rich he has sent empty away.*
> *   — Luke 1:46, 52-53*

It is true, of course, that Jesus' own Church since the days of Constantine has been often associated with the rich and powerful. If in Europe only five or ten percent of the population, even in Italy, attend church regularly, the church hierarchy is nonetheless often associated with the political powers. But in Latin America, many of the liberation theologians are using the teachings of Jesus and the writings of Karl Marx to break up the "interlocking directorate" of church hierarchy and state aristocracy. Gradually, through the base communities and various reforms, those of low degree are being exalted and the hungry are being fed.

It is to be remembered that much of Jesus' appeal was to those who were blamed too much in their time — people like prostitutes, tax collectors, sinners, peasants, neglected folk, and all the other multitudes of the great unwashed masses, the *hoi polloi*.

Blame had been carried too far. Were you blind? It was because you or your parents sinned, said the self-righteous. Were you epileptic or neurotic or even psychotic? You had a demon, said the authorities. Were you uneducated and dirt poor? That's your divinely appointed lot in life, said the aristocrats and oligarchs.

But the Heavenly Star Thrower gave them something to fix their minds on, to lift them up, to draw them up to a greater self-image and a higher estimate of self-worth when the powers-that-be were carrying blame too far.

That's why totalitarians of every age resist widespread distribution of the Bible in the people's language, because the Bible is a revolutionary book. It says each individual, no matter how lowly, is of infinite worth. It assures all the down-and-out of God's love and his intent to exalt them to wholeness and well-being.

But high or low in the world, this Star of Bethlehem, this Jesus, has placed high and lofty ideals before us and above us to inspire us.

> *Ideals are like stars; you will*
> *not succeed in touching them with*
> *your hands. But like the seafaring*
> *men on the desert of waters, you choose*

*them as your guides, and following them
you will reach your destiny,*

said Carl Scharz, in an address in Faneuil Hall in Boston, 1859.

To all those trapped in circumstance and landlocked in blame, the Star of Bethlehem inspires adventure with John Masefield, when he writes:

*I must go down to the seas again,
  to the lonely sea and sky,
And all I ask is a tall ship
  and a star to steer her by....*
— "Sea-Fever"

But this Star of Bethlehem, this Jesus who becomes the Christ, beckons to all the defeated, the depressed, the downtrodden, the discouraged, the disheartened, the dispossessed, the displaced, the diseased, the distressed, the disabled, the distraught of every generation — to all these the Christ beckons us to look skyward to the star, the fairest one in sight, because it asks of us a certain height,

*So when at times the mob is swayed
To carry praise or blame too far,
We may choose something like a star
To stay our minds on and be staid.*

If the Star Thrower intends to humble the proud and arrogant, perhaps he intends even more to exalt the humble and handicapped. At the recent Special Olympics in Seattle for those with physical and mental disabilities, the youngsters were lined up at the starting line for the 100-yard dash.

The starting gun was fired, and they were off — all except one, who stumbled and fell, and tumbled over a couple of times and began to cry. The other eight heard him, and turned back to help him. One girl with Down's Syndrome bent over and kissed him and said, "This will make it better." Then all nine handicapped children linked arms and walked together to the finish line. The stadium crowd stood and cheered and cheered and cheered. God intends to exalt all those of "low degree."

Oh yes, Heavenly Star Thrower, we have seen his Star in the East, and we have come to worship him with our gold, frankincense, and myrrh,

> *So when at times the mob is swayed*
> *To carry praise or blame too far,*
> *We may choose something like a star*
> *To stay our minds on and to be staid.*

Prayer

Eternal God, loving Father, from whose being has come the whole family of humankind, and by whose power we have been brought forth in your image upon the earth, we gather in this sacred space as children returning to the parent's home to honor and adore you, and to be reminded of who we are and whence we have come.

It is in your nature to welcome us back, despite our neglectfulness and prodigality. Once we have turned away from the far country you always come down the road to greet us and to affirm us as your own. We love you, O God, and are glad we are included and accepted into your family.

In this season of coming home and getting together, we bring before you the longings of our hearts for harmony and reconciliation. So often the strains and stresses of daily living harden our hearts and distract our minds. We are easily diverted down dark roads of doubt and forgetfulness. Those closest to us are readily taken for granted, and the helpful friends along life's way are allowed to fade into the background.

Speak to us anew this season, loving Father. As we draw closer to you, make us more thoughtful of one another. Save us from the anxiety of always having to be the favorite son or daughter. Release us from the compulsion always to demand from you and others and never to give. Enlarge our souls so at least to embrace anew those nearest and dearest.

Father of us all, speak in fatherly tones to the recalcitrant and wayward. Grant your tender compassion to those who mourn and your healing power to those ill in hospitals struggling with the powers of disease. And we pray for those in all sorts and conditions — for all children lost and alone, for families fractured by divorce or alienated by present offense or remembered grudge, for immigrants and strangers in the land, for the homeless and unemployed, for the soldiers far from home soon to be in harm's way, and for all souls longing for assurance that love's labor is not lost — for all these and more, we lift our ardent prayers to you, Loving Father of all the human family, that in your great wisdom and mercy you might grant our requests. Through Jesus Christ our Lord. Amen.

Chapter 8

The Inner Galaxy

And while they were there, the time came for her to be delivered. And she gave birth to her firstborn son and wrapped him in swaddling cloths, and laid him in a manger, because there was no place for them in the inn.
— Luke 2:6-7

Christmas Eve is the night for midnight blue skies, cloudless and serene; a night for stars dazzling and tantalizingly close to earth in all their silent glory; the night for galaxies vast and mysterious, drawing us away in time and space to worlds beyond the fringes of sense and imagination.

Increasingly urban as we are, we often lose the appreciation for the sky's nighttime splendor so spectacular to dwellers in the more arid climes. As a very young child in Wisconsin, on our way to the school Christmas program, I was entranced by the splendid glory of the winter sky. Through the years the wonder has never diminished and has grown even more as now we read of galaxies and stars in the making as viewed through the Hubble telescope. These galaxies, vast beyond description, distant beyond imagination, lure the mind and soul toward the edges of the infinite and beyond.

Robert Frost spoke of it when he wrote:

As I came to the edge of the woods,
Thrush music — hark!
Now if it was dusk outside,
Inside it was dark.

Too dark in the woods for a bird
By sleight of wing
To better its perch for the night,
Though it still could sing.

> *The last of the light of the sun*
> *That had died in the west*
> *Still lived for one song more*
> *In a thrush's breast.*
>
> *Far in the pillared dark*
> *Thrush music went —*
> *Almost like a call to come in*
> *To the dark and lament.*
>
> *But no, I was out for stars:*
> *I would not come in.*
> *I meant not even if asked,*
> *And I hadn't been.*
>   —"Come In"

Naturalist Loren Eiseley relates a similar experience in his youth, a time when he was out for stars, his attempt not only to examine the universe with the naked eye, but to observe the stars and galaxies through an observatory telescope on a mountain peak. The attempt to examine and explore outer space led him to turn his thoughts in the opposite direction, toward inner space. He observed "that the venture into space is meaningless unless it coincides with a certain interior expansion, an ever growing universe within to correspond with the far flight of the galaxies our telescopes follow from without" (*The Unexpected Universe*, p. 174).

Dr. Eiseley goes on to observe that "the inward skies of man will accompany him across any void upon which he ventures and will be with him to the end of time" (Eiseley, p. 175). It is true that Christmas Eve is about external galaxies — the star of Bethlehem, the heavenly hosts of angels singing, "Peace on earth, good will toward men," with the universe in the background as the stage props.

When we look into this sacred nighttime sky we are to be reminded there are something like a million billion billion planets in the universe. If all the science writers in the world were to shovel sand nonstop they couldn't shovel a million billion billion grains of sand in a lifetime, says Timothy Ferris in his book, *The Mind's Sky*. Add to that the fact that the universe of today is displayed across ten billion trillion trillion cubic light years of space after expanding from a hot little spark smaller than an atom — or so say some astrophysicists (Ferris, p. 84).

Yes, Christmas Eve does draw us outward and upward toward the vast, the infinite, the external and immeasurable, and we are out for stars. But perhaps even more, Christmas Eve draws us downward and inward toward the finite and internal. If outer galaxies dazzle us, inner galaxies intrigue us. If outer galaxies humble us, inner galaxies lift us up and affirm our self-worth. If outer galaxies have to do with eons and eons of time and trillions and trillions of light years of unconscious space, inner galaxies have to do with this particular time and this particular space.

The story is told of Teddy Roosevelt entertaining guests at his Sagamore Hill estate on Long Island. After a late dinner he invited his guests outside to walk beneath the brilliant nighttime sky. After a silent, reverent stroll Roosevelt said, "I guess we've been humbled enough now. Let's go inside."

And that's what Christmas Eve is all about — about stargazing toward the infinite to be humble in our finiteness. So in response to the angel chorus and the angel announcement, the simple, rustic, stargazing shepherds said, "Let us go even now into Bethlehem to see this thing that has happened...." And they went inside the stable, and beheld in the manger the inner galaxy — the interior meaning of the universe. And what did they experience?

I

For one thing, **they experienced mystery**. Luke tells us they returned "glorifying and praising God for all they had heard and seen...."

Writer Alan McGlashan says, "There is strong archeological evidence to show that with the birth of human consciousness there was born, like a twin, the impulse to transcend it." Indeed, that has been the experience of the prophets and poets and mystics of the centuries. When we come to behold both the outer and the inner galaxies we are startled by mystery. Whether it is Moses and the voice of God from the burning bush, or Isaiah caught up in a religious trance in the incense-filled Temple, or Jeremiah trembling with the inner Word of God, or the shepherds amazed in the presence of angels and Jesus, people through the ages have been awakened by mystery.

Sometimes the experience of nature does it. Poet William Wordsworth wrote of it at age eighteen:

> *And I have felt*
> *A presence that disturbs me with the joy*
> *Of elevated thoughts; a sense sublime*
> *Of something far more deeply interfused,*
> *Whose dwelling is the light of setting suns ...*
> *A motion and a spirit, that impels*
> *All thinking things, all objects of all thought,*
> *And rolls through all things....*
> — Lines Composed A Few Lines Above Tintern Abbey

William Blake experienced it when he wrote,

> *To see a world in a grain of sand*
> *And a heaven in a wild flower,*
> *Hold infinity in your hand*
> *And Eternity in a hour.*

Or it can be delightfully expressed as in the *Children's Letters To God*, this one by Eugene. He says: "Dear God: I didn't think orange went with purple until I saw the sunset you made on Tuesday. That was *cool*."

If nature suggests mystery, so does human nature. Famous Harvard psychologist, William James, wrote of the universal pervasiveness of the mystical experience without respect to specific religions or cultures or races. Consider the experience of Thomas Aquinas, theologian par excellence of the thirteenth century. Aquinas had revived the classics, especially Aristotle. He wrote prolifically, including his *Summa Theologica*, which is the standard theological work for the Roman Catholic Church today. Aquinas became enlightened with mystery while saying Mass in Naples, December 6, 1273. He ended his sermon, declaring, "I can do no more; such things have been revealed to me that all I have written seems as straw, and I now await the end of my life" (quoted in Ferris, p. 89).

Some years ago a man boasted to me of his extensive travels, impressive education, and vast experience, and that as a consequence he was convinced there was nothing new under the sun. How sad, I thought. How tragic to enclose yourself in such a prison. But then again, many of us get in that mood from time to time.

So then tonight, let us with the shepherds bow the knee to mystery. Let us with the poets and prophets, physicists and philosophers, theologians and hardened rationalists, humble ourselves with the shepherds to be open to mystery which transforms the inner galaxy.

II

What did the shepherds experience this magical night? **They experienced hope** — hope for peace on earth, good will toward men.

The story is told of two farmers conversing in a nineteenth century country general store in Kentucky. The general store was the place to exchange gossip and get caught up on the news. One farmer asked the other, "Anything new happening?" "Naw, not much," replied the other. "Except I hear Tom and Mary Lincoln had a baby boy. Named him Abraham. Not much going on."

So Caesar Augustus of imperial Rome could have said of this night long ago. King Herod was more anxious and killed all the Judean boys under two just to make sure nothing new would be going on. Even now with hundreds of births occurring every hour we are tempted to say not much is going on, except when it is our own child or grandchild.

The world's first birth ever is the birth of your own child. Except maybe in the case of little Joyce in her letter to God, where she said, "Dear God: Thank you for the baby brother, but what I prayed for was a puppy." Or possibly in little Marsha's letter to God where she wrote: "Dear God: My brother told me about being born, but it doesn't sound right" (*Children's Letters to God*).

And yet, even with all the births (all of them miraculous), even with Jesus' birth, many remain hopeless. They remain hopeless, says anthropologist Loren Eiseley, because they see man as the "brawling ape and bestial fighter" struggling for existence. All these births bring more of the same, say the pessimists — a human being controlled by dark passions and bloody instincts, a human being who is at heart a savage beast.

But all that's out of date, says anthropologist Eiseley. No materialistic reductionism can explain humanity. The direction for seeing our true nature is not so much backward as forward. Unlike lower creatures, we are not locked into our impulses and instincts. We keep redefining and reconceptualizing who we are and what we can become. Our psychological make-up is not fixed. We can see visions and dream dreams. The music Mozart heard in his head is soon played by orchestras and experienced by millions. The ideas which come from above and from within are soon architectural wonders or splendid works of art.

That is why Leonardo da Vinci could say, "I have offended God and mankind because my work didn't reach the quality it should have." Or why Claude Monet could say, "My life has been nothing but a failure." They always saw more than they could express.

Human beings have a restless inner eye, a capacity to transcend even their darkest selves, to give wings to their vision, form to their dreams, and structure to their altruism. "I am resigned to wait out man's long barbarity," says Eiseley. For Eiseley, with the shepherds and mystics on this holy night, has looked into the inner galaxy, into the dream world, into the visions of things yet to be. And with the shepherds he has hope — because we have seen in Jesus more than we have ever yet been able to express.

III

But even more, the shepherds on this night **experienced love**.

If anything can awaken love and admiration, it is a baby. On a crowded department store elevator the other day, a young mother entered with her beautiful, smiling baby. The once silent, reserved elevator crowd began cooing and smiling and kitchee-kitchee cooing as if on cue. And all that from only one floor to another! Is it any wonder actors hate to act with babies? They upstage even a Robert Redford or a Demi Moore.

God has designed human beings to procreate by the act and ecstasy of love — an appropriate way for beginning that miraculous, new inner galaxy of an embryo and human being. For the body itself is an inner galaxy — the womb and the fetus growing within it — a galaxy of endless wonder and miracle.

Writer Harriet Ritchie tells the story of her family searching out a nearly deserted truckstop after the Christmas Eve midnight service for a Christmas breakfast. The air smelled of coffee, bacon, and stale cigarette smoke. A one-armed man in a baseball cap was drinking Pepsi from a bottle at the counter. Two other men sat at a table talking and eating on a lonely night.

The thin, weary waitress came to take their orders. Then an old, overloaded Volkswagen came. A young couple got out with their little baby, and took a booth in the back. The baby wouldn't stop crying, and the embarrassed young mother started to leave. The waitress said, "Here, let me see what I can do. You drink your coffee."

She talked and cooed, showed the baby to the one-armed man who began whistling and making funny faces to make the baby stop crying. As Rita, the waitress, took the baby to explore the blinking lights, the one-armed man took coffee from a burner and began waiting on tables. And a warm glow came over the whole scene.

Harriet Ritchie said she was moved to tears and said to her husband, "If Jesus were born tonight in this town, he'd come here to this truckstop, wouldn't he, rather than to our upscale neighborhood and church?" "Either here or a homeless shelter," said her husband.

But then as they were getting into the car her husband added, "Remember the angel said, 'I bring good news of great joy to *all* people.' " And Harriet Ritchie remembered the needy people in her upscale neighborhood, and I remembered our neighborhood.

Over here is a family whose house burned down with a mother and child inside. Over there is an athlete and attorney with Lou Gehrig's disease, who breathes with a ventilator and talks through a computer. Over here is a woman whose aged father had died — a father for whom she cared and with whom she had become an adult friend. Over there is a young man about to have a malignant tumor removed from a lung. Over here is a woman whose husband left her and the three children for another woman. Over there is a man whose business of ten years failed in an economic downturn. Over here is a mother whose little six-year-old girl has incurable cancer.

Does Jesus come only to homeless shelters and deserted truckstops on Christmas Eve? "No," says the angel. "I bring good news of great joy to *all* people." And it is the news of a love that never gives up, news of a love that transforms inner galaxies and causes a generous outpouring of money and talent and helpfulness to all in need.

This love which sets everything in motion, as Aristotle said, is the same love that moves the sun and stars along, said Dante, and is the same love however discounted in our time, which, says scientist and naturalist Eiseley, "moved the dying Christ on Golgotha with a power that has reached across two thousand weary years" (Eiseley, *op. cit.*, p. 179).

And now it is for us on this holy night, to bow the knee in adoration, and to open the door wide to our inner galaxy, where mystery waits to ignite a cold mind, and where hope beckons to a defeated spirit, and where most of all, love would flood our inner beings with love for God and love for one another.

So with Phillips Brooks we pray:

> *O holy child of Bethlehem*
> *Descend to us, we pray;*
> *Cast out our sin and enter in;*
> *Be born in us today.*
> *We hear the Christmas angels*
> *The great glad tidings tell;*
> *O come to us, abide with us,*
> *Our Lord Emmanuel.*

Prayer

Eternal God, who calls the stars into being and who makes sport with galaxies and who expresses yourself in universes beyond our comprehending, it was your pleasure at the beginning of time to brood over the primeval waters and to bring forth light and life upon the earth. You visited our planet with your presence to shape us in your image and to bring your very being to self-expression in us as your people. We praise and adore you for the fathomless mysteries of the universe, and thank you that you have brought us into the adventure of living, loving, and thinking, as a part of your grand scheme of things entire toward which the whole creation moves.

Visit us again tonight with an awakened sense of your holiness and power, and quicken our minds toward the new realities you have in store for us. The world is very much with us, late and soon. The burdens of life often oppress. The pressures and stress tax our resources and nearly exhaust our inner reserve. So be pleased to refresh us, O God, for the living of these days.

On this night of miraculous birth, we pray you will cause us to be reborn from within. Some of us have had seeds of creative thoughts needing germination. Some have had new inventions brooding within their minds for a better world. Some have had dreams for economic justice and greater equity for the poor and oppressed.

Others of us have had glimmers of ideas for love better expressed in our families and we have received hints of ways of forgiving grudges so long and firmly held. In others of us there is the book or poem to be written, the music to be composed, the business to be formed, the kindly word to be said, the generous gift to be given, the friendly deed to be done. O God, bring to birth all the latent creativity within and the residual potential buried beneath our fears.

And hear us, loving Father, as we make our supplication for peace on earth, good will toward men. Remove the strife within our families. Cause us to bridge the generation gap and other gaps — the gaps of race and language, culture and religion. Bring contentment to ravaged souls. Heal those torn by hatred and violence. Comfort those who mourn, and grant your healing power to all those who do battle with the powers of disease in body, mind, and soul.

Thank you, God, for this night, for Jesus the Christ, your Word became flesh among us, full of grace and truth. Through Jesus Christ our Lord. Amen.

Chapter 9

The Second Naiveté: Babies, Angels, Shepherds, And God

And being found in human form he humbled himself and became obedient unto death, even death on a cross.
— Philippians 2:8

You would have liked him as did thousands, perhaps millions. He was engaging, intriguing, brilliant, and humorous. Had you met him on the street you probably would not have guessed who he was — a businessman possibly, even a taxi driver. But as a leading scientist he was known to thousands through his popular television series, *The Ascent of Man*, later developed into a marvelous book of the same title. His name? Jacob Bronowski.

I first heard Jacob Bronowski in Minnesota at a college conference on creativity. On a cold January day with crisp snow and a lowering grey sky outside, on the inside, Bronowski emitted a warm glow and radiance with his speech. Students and professors alike were drawn to him not only by his brilliance, but also by his charm and genuine humility. Accustomed to audiences of thousands, he spoke to this audience of hundreds as though it were the only audience in the world. He was really there, present with us, provocative and engaging.

And ironically and strangely, it was this brilliant scientist, the pioneer on the frontiers of human knowledge, who suggested we should approach reality — all reality — with a sense of wonder and awe, and an attitude of humility and even naiveté. "We need," suggested Bronowski, "a kind of second naiveté, a renewed, childlike innocence and openness to advance to new levels of understanding and insight."

"There was a time — and a recent time at that," says Bronowski, "when scientists were less than humble. Confident they were on the verge of discovering the very core of Reality itself, they presumed to be close to explaining everything, at least everything that mattered.

"But no longer," asserts Bronowski. "All our information is imperfect. We have to treat it with humility. We have a paradox of knowledge," says the late Salk Institute scientist. At the very time scientists devise instruments more and more precise by which to observe nature, they discover the observations are fuzzy and that scientists are as uncertain as ever. Says Bronowski, "We seem to be running after a goal which lurches away from us to infinity every time we come within sight of it" (*The Ascent of Man*, p. 356). Consequently, we need to approach reality with awe and wonder and humility. We need, Bronowski might say, a second naiveté by which to see.

Another scientist and historian of science would, in his own way, agree. And for this scientist we move from the Salk Institute in LaJolla, California, on the West Coast, to the East Coast's Harvard University, and one-time professor Thomas Kuhn.

A few years ago, Kuhn published a book titled *The Structure of Scientific Revolutions* — a book that has had a significant impact on the philosophy of science and knowing. "How do scientific revolutions come about?" Kuhn asked himself in research. They often come about through anomalies, that is, through things that seem unusual or out of place. Anomalies do not fit into the accepted order of things and often are dismissed or ignored in research.

Dismissed or ignored, that is, by those who already have their minds made up. But to younger scientists, to those perhaps a little more curious or humble, the anomaly often proves to be an entirely new way of perceiving reality. Through a kind of second naiveté, what heretofore was ignored is observed by the open, inquiring mind. And very often a major paradigm shift occurs, something like the Copernican revolution. And as a consequence, we have a new way of seeing and understanding. It is the gift of the second naiveté.

I

Christmas Eve is not only the night of the Holy Nativity. It is also, we might say, the night of the Holy Naiveté, the Second Naiveté.

Of course, few of us would want anything to do with the first naiveté. Sophisticated, city-hardened, sensuously sated New Yorkers can spot country bumpkins of the first naiveté a mile away. Wherever they are from, New Yorkers know these stereotypical, gawking, guileless gullibles are from somewhere else. And New Yorkers inwardly thank themselves that they are shrewder, sharper, and far more worldly and cosmopolitan than these straightforward types from the West.

But these so-called sappy Westerners are only too happy to get even when the New Yorkers venture beyond the Hudson to the wild unknown of a dude ranch or a big game hunting expedition in the mountains. "You don't like the bears and beans up here, buster?" asks the wiry-muscled, leather-skinned trail boss at 8,000 feet. "Well then, just catch yourself a taxi and go back home."

Naive people? We see them everywhere. Want to insult someone? Call them naive. Probably nothing cuts to the quick faster than being called naive, by which they mean gullible, credulous, unsophisticated, provincial; innocent, inexperienced, and unacquainted with the ways of the world.

And when you think of it, sometimes naive people can be a bit much. In face of the world's grinding wretchedness, they exhibit a kind of giddy simplicity. In a society interlaced with duplicity and intrigue, they surge into the playing field like a rabbit in front of greyhounds. Within a humanity besieged with evil and suffering, and within human flesh stalked by disease and death, these naive wonderlings hold forth an optimism that is at once amazing and obnoxious. And to make matters worse, these babies in naive-land don't even know they are naive.

Naiveté? No thanks. We prefer to be cosmopolitan, sophisticated, worldly-wise, skeptical, distrusting; critical, reserved, cautious, calculating, distant, and unbelieving. We'll be cool, thank you. You play the fool. We'll be coy, thank you. You can be the ploy. We'll be the sated; you be the simple. We'll be the controllers;

you be the controlled. We'll make the money; you do the work. You want to change the world? We'll be content to let the world work in our favor.

Naiveté? No thanks.

II

So much for the first naiveté. Let's come back to the second naiveté. In many ways, that is what this night of the Holy Nativity is all about — about a second way of seeing and knowing, about a second look at something we might have missed before, an insight into an "anomaly" ignored by the sophisticated and worldly-wise, but seen by those with eyes to see and ears to hear.

And who are these of the second naiveté? In the Christmas story they are the shepherd and the astrologer, both of them stargazers, both of them spending long nights absorbing the brilliant desert sky, both of them contemplating mysteries and wonders beyond the ordinary and beyond our control. We city-dwellers find the nighttime sky blocked by our own city lights. Our own minimal brilliance blocks the transcendent galaxies and the splendor of an infinite space.

Have we seen it all? Not so, say the shepherds and innocent lambs. Have we got a grasp on all the significant realities? Not so, say the angels and wise men. Does our worldly wisdom pretty much have it summed up? Look again, says Saint Paul. The foolishness of God is wiser than the wisdom of men, and the weakness of God vastly more powerful than the power of men. "There is a sense," says Paul, "in which God himself has exhibited a second naiveté toward the world."

God keeps coming into the world through lawgivers and prophets, through artists and musicians, through wise and holy people, and God seems to be ignored. Through his messengers, his angels, God says one thing, and people do another.

You would think by now that God would have learned his lesson. Doesn't he know people can't be trusted? Haven't the atrocities of the human race registered with him? Doesn't he remember what first brother Cain did to second brother Abel? Has he forgotten Sodom and Gomorrah? Has he overlooked the

Armenian massacre, the Gulag Archipelago, the Holocaust, and the blood-baths of Cambodia's Pol Pot regime? Has God read the tabloids or does he peruse only the news that is fit to print? Is God naive, or what?

Not naive, says Paul, but exceedingly humble and kind. Not naive, says Paul, but patient and forgiving. Not naive, says Paul, but willing to take a chance again on humanity, and to take a chance this time not so much on Moses or Isaiah or Jeremiah, but to take a chance in one he would come to call his very Son, Jesus of Mary and Joseph; Jesus, an innocent, vulnerable, helpless infant born in a Bethlehem stable. Jesus, a very human baby, at risk — greatly at risk in a world cold and callous and scornful of innocence and naiveté.

But I tell you the miracle of a baby will get people on their knees faster than the monarchs or potentates. Presidents and executives and prestigious doctors and lawyers and ministers can be found all over the world humbling themselves before the miracle of a child or grandchild. And when God decided to favor a special child, shepherds adored him, kings gave him gifts, and even the angels sang.

After all is said and done, is God brash and arrogant, callous and aloof, proud and pompous? Does God adorn himself in peacock plumage and look upon the world with distant hauteur? Does God, in all his power and glory, sneer at our pretensions of power and scoff at our pathetic attempts at utopian glory?

No, says Paul. He looks at us with a kind of second naiveté. He empties himself of his glory and puts himself at risk in humanity again, making himself vulnerable, again, in a baby he hopes will be a new model man of obedience in place of the old model man, Adam, who failed with disobedience. And it was this baby, this Jesus, God's chosen second naiveté, who humbled himself and became obedient unto death, even death on a cross.

God will go to any lengths to waken us again to his higher reality, his deeper love, his steadfast patience with the human race, even if it takes a kind of second naiveté on his part.

But then, of course, it takes a second naiveté on our part. "Our heroic images we create for ourselves tend to be rather crude," says Jacob Bronowski. "But," says Bronowski, "the real vision of the human being is the child wonder, the Virgin and Child, the Holy Family" (p. 425).

Yes, that is the real vision — the vision of the second naiveté — God's and ours. It is the vision of understanding, forgiving, eternal love. God doesn't browbeat us into submission. Instead he comes to us in humble, tender, suffering love. And as a consequence, we are lost in wonder, love, and praise.

Glory to God in the highest (and lowest) and on earth, peace, goodwill to men! Alleluia! Amen!

Prayer

Eternal God, Lord of all the universe, Creator of all galaxies and solar systems, and our Creator, we come to you with wonder and adoration. In all your majesty and power you have come to us so humbly, so gently and tenderly, with such patient love.

As long ago you visited Bethlehem with light and love and inspired the worship of shepherds and the adoration of wise men, so too visit us, and awaken our minds and heart to new realities we have been too busy or too conceited to see.

God of this night's stillness and peace, who reigns over the stars and guides the way to the Prince of Peace; so lead us anew to the manger to behold the Christ. We confess our fascination with the world of time and sense, pomp and circumstance. But on this night of humble love and eternal truth, help us give up the idols of our vain worship, to center our lives on the Christ. Grant us release from false ideas and inadequate concepts which hinder our vision of you. Let our hardness of heart be melted in the warmth of this manger room of love.

On this night of the world's first family, we would remember our own. Some of us are home from school or service or distant work. Others of us are home after arguments and alienation, home, ready to be accepted and reconciled. As the coming of Christ bound Mary and Joseph together in love, so may his coming bind our families together in new warmth and affection. Let us have your blessing of a new family life of integrity and thoughtfulness. Cleanse our souls with fond memories, and gladden our hearts with the promise of a new day.

On this night of humble, but noble birth, we would remember all women in labor, all mothers with children of promise, all fathers with responsibility for shaping sacred life. Bless them and us with wisdom, we pray.

On this night of no room in the inn, we pray for all travelers and wanderers without shelter and food and clothing, for all pilgrims of mind and soul, that they may come to dwell in you. Make us agents of mercy and messengers of good will. Through Jesus Christ our Lord. Amen.

Bibliography

Bach, Richard, *Jonathan Livingston Seagull*, New York, New York, Macmillan, 1970.

Bronowski, Jacob, *The Ascent of Man*, Boston, Massachusetts, Little, Brown and Company, 1973.

Eiseley, Loren, *The Star Thrower*, New York, New York, Harcourt Brace Jovanovich, 1978.

Eiseley, Loren, *The Invisible Pyramid*, London, England, Rupert Hart-Davis, 1971.

Eiseley, Loren, *The Unexpected Universe*, New York, New York, Harcourt Brace Jovanovich, 1969.

Ferris, Timothy, *The Mind's Sky*, New York, New York, Bantam Books, 1992.

Frost, Robert, *The Road Not Taken*, New York, New York, Henry Holt & Company, 1971.

The Gospel According to John I-XII, Anchor Bible, Garden City, New York, Doubleday, Inc., 1966.

Hample, Stuart and Marshall, Eric, *Children's Letters To God*, New York, New York, Workman, 1991.

Heschel, Abraham, *The Prophets*, New York, New York, Harper & Row, 1962.

James, William, *The Varieties of Religious Experience*, New York, New York, Random House, 1929.

Kazantzakis, Nikos, *The Last Temptation of Christ*, New York, New York, Simon & Schuster, Inc. 1960.

Kuhn, Thomas S. *The Structure of Scientific Revolutions*, Chicago, Illinois, University of Chicago Press, 1962.

Renan, Ernest, *The Life of Jesus*, Buffalo, New York, Prometheus Books, 1991.

Schonfield, Hugh, *The Passover Plot*, New York, New York, Bantam Books, Inc. 1969.

Shea, John, *The Challenge of Jesus*, Garden City, New York, Doubleday, 1977.

Williams, Daniel Day, *The Spirit and the Forms of Love*, New York, New York, Harper & Row, 1968.

www.ingramcontent.com/pod-product-compliance
Lightning Source LLC
Chambersburg PA
CBHW071733040426
42446CB00012B/2345